OPEN DOORS

STORIES FROM WILDLIFE NATION

ALL PROCEEDS FROM THE SALE OF THIS BOOK WILL GO TO

BENEFIT WILDLIFENATION.ORG

OPEN DOORS

STORIES FROM WILDLIFE NATION

Table of Contents

Introduction

An Intimate Connection
Diane Lefer   Pg 11

How One Short Hike can Leave a Permanent Trace
David Weinstock   Pg 17

Perpetual Outsider
Tamara Dean   Pg 21

Watching the Eagle Fly
Becky Lentz   Pg 29

Labrador
Kiley Pratt   Pg 32

The Magic of the Outdoors
Bill Dodge   Pg 37

Apples
William Luginbuhl   Pg 41

Mountains to Climb
Tessa Fancher   Pg 47

Rookery Roots
Greg Seitz   Pg 50

Unlearning Bad Habits
Jenny Montagne   Pg 57

Apology
Lené Gary   Pg 64

Growing Up Outdoors in Michigan
Elvera Shappirio   Pg 69

Nature's Laws
Isaac Yelchin   Pg 74

Choosing When to Let Go
Carla Brown   Pg 78

Out the Door
Mary Fancher   Pg 81

Alley Games
Barbara Debrodt   Pg 90

Inheriting an Outdoor Life
Eugenie Doyle   Pg 93

Early Morning Walks
Kathleen McKinley Harris   Pg 95

Passion
Jan Hudson Krueger   Pg 98

River Ride
Kitty Rogers   Pg 104

I Love to Ski
Kirsty Stevenson   Pg 107

Revolution Summer
Nick Chedli Carter   Pg 113

Why I Love To Be Outdoors
Pauline Loewenhardt   Pg 117

Digging, Beaching, and Spending Time with Those I Love
Peggy Howard   Pg 125

The Wild West In Four Parts
Sean McNamara   Pg 130

Afoot
Sally W. Buffington   Pg 142

Summer Camp at Medokawanda
Joey Lincoln   Pg 150

Gravity, Grief and Gratitude
Barbara Miles   Pg 154

You Can't Catch a Fish Without a Line in the Water
Paul Fancher   Pg 163

Writers and the War Against Nature
Gary Snyder   Pg 195

INTRODUCTION

When we first bought our little piece of property in upstate New York we stayed in tents. There was a house, but the woman who had been living there had let bats own the upstairs. She had boarded up the stairway and let them multiply while she lived downstairs. I don't know how many of the 50 years she lived there she allowed that to happen, but when we started to tear down walls, what looked like insulation was bat guano. Tons and tons of guano. We called it the bat house and debated the wisdom of renovating or simply tearing it down. Mostly we stayed outside, away from the smell. And we camped.

Luckily I love to camp. We pitched our tents on a point of land right by the water. That spot was – is – an eighth of a mile from the end of our dirt road. There aren't streetlights. There aren't cars. There aren't services - wifi or cell or 3G. Nothing. It's dark and when something moves in that dark it sounds like a ten-ton gorilla. We lay in our tents many nights and listened while giant unknowable things jumped into the water. Sometimes we ventured out on the rocks unable to see anything but the distant stars.

In the daylight we swam and kayaked and canoed. We fished. We watched snakes and birds and dragonflies and beavers. Once I watched as three young turtles crawled out of a hole, looked at each other, then turned in three different directions and moved away in such perfectly orchestrated precision that it had to have been planned.

Over time we renovated and aerated the bat house and began to stay in it on our overnights. It was so private and so peaceful; when we were there all of time went away. We joked that we needed a place to get away from the stress of living in Vermont. And even though we lived in a rural village and our kids spent many hours - many unsupervised hours - outdoors, this was a place that felt important. It felt needed in their lives. A place with a million distractions and none of them electronic.

Naturally our kids began to bring other kids – they brought skis and snowshoes, built ice sculptures on the rocks in the winter. In the summer they swam and hiked and had campfires. Having always believed that kids needed to be outdoors, were actually happiest outdoors, I began to organize camps. With a friend, I set up one week camps. Fourteen kids, everyone slept on the floor, everyone took turns cooking and cleaning. We had a structure of sorts to our days – yoga, writing, drawing, swimming, boating, story-telling. We added in hiking, soccer, talent shows, chase, washing your hair in a downpour, campfires, poetry reading, skits – as time and interest dictated.

It's hard to put into words what happened during those weeks. It has a tendency to sound cheesy and sappy and stick-your-finger-down-your-throat gaggy, but I saw people change. I saw kids – teens – relax and begin to trust that it was ok to be their goofiest selves. Or their creative selves, or their serious selves, or their caring selves.

One night we sat out in the dark, each kid on their own rock facing the lake. The frogs were singing in every key, the stars were out and glinting on the water. No one spoke. It was wind and stars and frogs and leaves rustling in the trees. Beavers and raccoons moved through the undergrowth. Bats whirled here and there. But no one moved. No one called out. No one complained of the mosquitoes. We just listened. I've had other moments swollen with emotion, I love my own children with a fierceness that borders on scary, but this moment was as perfect as a moment could be. It wasn't about nostalgia, there was no desire to keep the moment forever, just knowledge that, recognized in the moment or not, these kids were experiencing the best life could offer: acceptance, freedom to be themselves, a moment without pressure, a moment to be consciously part of the vast and unknowable universe. Not a moment to feel small, but to be part of something immense and beautiful and fleeting. We were the world and the world was us.

It was important to me that the kids that came to our camp find an appreciation for the outdoors. I wanted them to know what it was to be comfortable outside. I wanted them to know the outdoors because what you don't know, you can't treasure. And what you don't treasure, you don't protect. Even if, after the week, they returned to their cell phones and video games, they had this in them. It was there. It was a start.

What those kids had I want all kids to have. Not just kids, all people to have. I want them to feel connected to the outdoors, comfortable, interested, and concerned for the preservation of the planet. And that's where my connection to Wildlife Nation comes in. It's a wide-ranging outdoor and online community – an offspring of The National Wildlife Federation - aiming to inform and connect people with wildlife, people with outdoor activities, people with people, in a great act of sharing and exploration. Its aim is to bridge life in the cyber world with life in the greater world. And one of those ways is through the sharing of stories.

I asked 50 people of all ages, of differing professions and experiences, to tell a story of something they'd done, or experienced, or learned, or felt in nature, or about nature. It made for a pretty broad topic and the responses have been diverse. I was hoping for inspiration, for that spark that would make others want to get outside and try some of the same things. What I found was a whole chorus of voices who cared. Many of the 30 who responded did not consider themselves writers, but they wrote. For that I am grateful.

In reading the stories, it became clear to me that the themes of autonomy, independence, discovery, and freedom were crucial to these writers' sense of self. They needed to learn to do things for themselves, to make decisions independently, to trust their own abilities, to find solace in the outdoors on the days the world is harsh, to find joy in their own discoveries. The individual voices convinced me more than ever that everyone has a story to tell – at least one – worth listening to, and their own way of telling it. These stories do provide inspiration. I believe that sharing stories will help grow a community that cares about the fate of the world. Please enjoy them. Be inspired. Go outside. Take a kid with you.

- Janet Fancher

To learn more (and join!) Wildlife Nation please visit wildlifenation.org.

Diane Lefer

Diane Lefer is the author of 11 books including the award-winning short story collection, California Transit, *which takes place in part at the Marine Mammal Care Center in San Pedro. Her work is included in the Ashland Creek Press anthology* Among Animals. *Diane volunteers at the Amanda Foundation animal rescue and at the Los Angeles Zoo. More at www.dianelefer.weebly.com*

AN INTIMATE CONNECTION

As a New York City child, I lived in an apartment development that housed 25,000 people and not a single cat or dog. No pets allowed. One day, a woman who didn't know the rules showed up with two cocker spaniels and word spread as if by magic. Kids came pouring off the playgrounds and out of the buildings till she was surrounded, all of us shouting with joy, hoping to pet (or at least see) the dogs. Security guards had to break through and extricate her and the spaniels, moving them off the property and away from the mob.

Children hunger for the company of animals. I clucked at squirrels and watched the sparrows and starlings and fed the pigeons. Long before I started school, my father led me on long walks through the city, to streets where people did indeed freely walk their dogs – but *Don't try to pet them! You don't know if they're friendly!* – and to the East River piers in an era before redevelopment and pedestrian esplanades. We carried sardine sandwiches for lunch, appropriately fishy and smelly, to a picnic spot redolent of creosote and tar. The pilings creaked, rainbows shimmered in the oil on the surface of the brackish water and there were seagulls to swoop and dive and excite me with their piercing cries.

It wasn't enough. I had a nature book with pictures of North American birds. Barn Swallow, Cedar Waxwing, Goldfinch, Meadowlark, Rose-breasted Grosbeak, Scarlet Tanager, Snowy Egret. Someday, I insisted, I would get to see them all. In the meantime, I went around reciting their names. Baltimore Oriole, Magpie, Tufted Titmouse, Wren.

Robin. I knew the song about the *red red robin* and I'd seen them in picture books. The first time I saw one in real life, the most amazing sight thrilled me: the bird's head went down, the beak penetrated the earth, and up it came with a worm. It's hard to explain the startling wonder of that moment. Something I'd seen in pictures turned out to really happen in real life. It's as though until that moment Life had simply spun about around me and there was no point trying to make sense of it. But now I understood that what we learn about in a book is more than pictures and words. It's *real*. There was a point and purpose to *learning.*

For me, learning and Nature remain intimately connected.

I never became a true bird-watcher. I don't have a life list. But I've seen a red-tailed hawk plunge into a crevice in a rock face. In the alpine forest of New Mexico, with great beating of wings, a gray jay flew straight at me. Instinctively, my eyes blinked shut so that I first felt and only then saw the wild bird that landed on my hand. I've thrilled to parrots in the skies of Mexico and, visiting an ancient ruin in Turkey, was tickled to see a stork claim one of the great high pillars for its nest.

I'm still an urban dweller although it's different here in Los Angeles. Walking the city streets or crossing a parking lot you may well encounter skunk, opossum, even a coyote, while bobcats and mountain lions are spotted now and then in the hills and suburban swimming pools can prove irresistibly attractive to the occasional black bear.

There are hiking trails even within the city limits, intoxicating me with the fragrance of chaparral and coastal sage. Park rangers lead nighttime hikes where glowworms often light the way. The frogs sing in chorus and once I saw an owl plunge suddenly from the sky and just as suddenly strike and carry off its prey.

Outdoors in the great world, you never know who or what you'll find. There was the man from Peru who said what he most appreciates when visiting the U.S. is being able to hike in the wilderness. Crime and violence have made the trails outside of Lima no longer safe, he said. It hurts his heart that his children and grandchildren can't wander through the mountains as he once did. He reminded me to value what we have.

In the canyons, I came across a woman who showed off the tarantulas she'd let climb upon her arm.

"They have a bad reputation," she said, "but they're really gentle. Would you like to hold one?"

I was fascinated, but NO!

And just as I did with the names of the birds, I repeat the common names of the plants that grow wild: sweet memory skyflower, padre's shooting star, witch's hair, sticky monkey-flower.

My mind often stumbles over that last one. I find myself thinking "*stinky* monkey-flower," as I recall childhood visits to the old monkey house in the Central Park Zoo. No visit was complete unless you ventured inside, though it was hard to stay long amid the shrieking of the monkeys and, most of all, the stench. Back then, few people gave much thought to the animals' wellbeing. The monkeys' angry, distraught, *stinky* behavior was, as far as most visitors were concerned, completely natural.

We understand more now. The monkey house is gone from Central Park. In zoos all over the country, small concrete-floored prison cages are being replaced with natural habitats. Here in Los Angeles, where I've volunteered with the research department for 16 years, the gorillas, for example, live in the expansive Campo Gorilla Reserve complete with trees and grass and flowers, waterfalls, rocks to climb, with sunny areas as well as places dark with shade.

The research department studies and observes animal behavior to best understand the conditions that will keep the zoo animals healthy, both physically and psychologically. Keepers and the behavioral enrichment team promote natural behavior. Instead of just providing food, they hide tasty treats inside logs or other objects so that animals have to work at providing for themselves.

Visiting the zoo is much like hiking the outdoors. Narrow paths wind through 113 acres of palms, cacti and succulents, roses, bird of paradise, cape honeysuckle, African coral, and carob trees. The acacia, mulberry, eucalyptus, and giant fig trees furnish zoo residents with food, or "browse." Peacocks strut about and flap their way up to the tops of exhibits, and back down to sweep the ground with their tails and then fan them open in full splendor. As a volunteer, I'm sometimes privileged to wander about after sundown when night-blooming flowers perfume the air and coyotes who live free in the surrounding hills come down to see what there is to see – or eat. I wonder what they make of the cages.

I'm not sure what I make of the cages. For all of my commitment to the zoo, it pains me to see animals in captivity. But zoos today support conservation efforts here and around the world. During my first assignment – the drill baboon breeding project – I learned the drill is the world's most endangered primate. Their forest habitat in West Africa is disappearing due to logging operations; once the drills are forced out into the open, people kill them for bush meat.

As I observed the zoo's drills for months, I amassed quantifiable data but also learned these baboons can fall in love as tenderly and deeply as any human being – and not always with a reproductively capable mate.

I've learned that some nonhuman primates (or individuals) are as curious about people as we are about them, or able to ignore our presence at will. Not so the endangered red uakari monkey. It's hard for a zoo to justify keeping, feeding, and caring for animals that zoo visitors can't see, so for a few weeks, armed with clipboard and data collection forms, timer, and protocol, I set out to document behavior. If we found a strong correlation between disturbed or aggressive behavior and the presence of zoo visitors, we'd be able to make a case that the uakaris needed and deserved privacy. We found it; they got it. Today the uakaris climb and play in an area shielded from intruders and prying eyes.

We've also cared for animals that most likely would not otherwise have survived: a blind magpie, a bear cub orphaned by forest fire.

Then there was the magnificent Sumatran tiger who'd lived most of his life in a small bare enclosure. Now we were about to introduce him to his own little jungle, lush with foliage and palm trees and a moat. Unlike most cats, tigers in the wild are strong, enthusiastic swimmers but we understood the new arrival had never seen water deeper than in the shallow pan he drank from. I was sent to monitor him, armed with a walkie-talkie to call for help if he ventured into the moat and floundered.

My breath caught as he emerged from his cave. His striped body rippled as he raced past the palms and plunged directly into the water, swimming as though he'd done it all his life. In fact, I thought, he had been waiting all his life to do what comes naturally to a tiger.

The Devil's Punchbowl lures me to the high desert town of Pearblossom in the northern reaches of LA County. After I leave the car, I descend into the chasm, into a sandstone maze of tilted slabs and rounded weathered stone where kids shout and play hide-and-seek among the weird rock shapes. I love seeing families here and in the Nature Center and I'm grateful not only for this county park but because a new generation is learning to love it as I do. But today I'm in the mood for solitude.

I head for higher elevations, traveling along where a fragrant pinyon-juniper forest lines the bowl's rim, and higher still. The trail winds to one false summit and down again, then up to still another. A couple of hours more on the exposed slope, stopping again and again for water and sunscreen, and I'm out of breath. Then my goal is in sight. On the narrow ridge, steps cut out of stone lead to the perch I'm after.

From the Devil's Chair, I have a 360-degree view: the blue sky and San Gabriel Mountains as a backdrop to the frozen chaos of fantastical rock formations in the faultline canyons below. But as I sit in the sun and wind, I'm not thinking of geology. Or data collection or protocols. I'm thinking of nothing. Whatever the red robin taught me so many years ago is unlearned now. I'm back to a time before things had names. All I have are my senses. The world is here around me and I don't ask it to make sense. The beauty is enough and the majesty and the dizzying wordless joy.

David Weinstock

David Weinstock is a poet, essayist and creative writing teacher and formerly wrote catalog copy for L.L. Bean, West Marine, and the Orvis Company. He lives in Middlebury, Vermont, with his mountain-climbing, peak-bagging wife and two sons.

HOW ONE SHORT HIKE CAN LEAVE A PERMANENT TRACE

Many years later, as he faced the firing squad, Colonel Aureliano Buendía was to remember that distant afternoon when his father took him to discover ice.

–Gabriel Garcia Marquez, in One Hundred Years of Solitude

One July day in my seventh year, my father picked up the geologist's hammer he carried in the trunk of his car, rounded up the family – my mother, my younger brother, and me – and led us on a nature hike into the woods behind our house.

We lived in southern New Jersey, in a town called Vineland. Vineland had been founded a century before by Charles K. Landis as a planned utopian community. Such ventures usually go bad, but Vineland prospered, even after 1876 when Mr. Landis shot and killed Uri Carruth, the town's newspaper editor.

Now, who hasn't wanted to do that and never quite followed through? But Charles Landis was a man of action who got things done.

17

Vineland was not the first or only town he founded. He was a serial town founder, leaving us Hammonton, Sea Isle City, Landisville and Millville. He had some progressive ideas. Landis believed in open spaces and laid out his new town with a grid of tree-lined streets, mandating deep setbacks in front of the houses and ample wooded space behind. We owned seven acres of pine, oak and sassafras, which made my father happy.

Local historians, ever concerned with civic pride, dance around the embarrassing fact of the murder. When forced to address the subject, to salvage Vineland's honor, they assert that, always a groundbreaker, Landis was the first murder defendant ever to be acquitted with the defense of temporary insanity. This is not exactly true; the dubious honor belongs to a congressman, Daniel Sickles, who in 1859 killed a United States district attorney. But back to the hike.

We walked to the edge of the forest, but before we plunged in, my father approached a pine tree, lifted his hammer and with the chisel end ripped a vertical slash through the bark into the white wood below. He said he was blazing the trail, and as the hike went on, Dad marked more trees, every twenty or thirty yards.

Decades later when I told this to my wife, a modern Appalachian Trail hiker, she rolled her eyes. Today's eco-conscious stewards of the earth have a "Leave No Trace" ethos that forbids such desecration. If a trail absolutely must be blazed, the fashion is to apply discreet vertical stripes of white or blue paint, and as few as possible of those. One blaze every 500 feet is considered quite enough for ordinary trails; in designated wilderness areas blazes are supposed to be even farther apart.

It was a nature hike, and my father knew his trees. He showed us how the sassafras trees had four different shapes of leaves: oval, left mitten, right mitten, and three thumbs. Then he pulled up a sassafras seedling and peeled the fragrant bark from its roots for me to smell. "Just like root beer," he said.

Dad pointed out oak trees, but would not be more specific, literally: he would not venture a guess about which species a particular tree belonged to. He quoted his old forestry professor at Rutgers who had said, "Only a fool would try to identify an oak!"

He also showed us moss, scooping up a clump of the dark green carpet. The sand underneath was bleached white, what they call "sugar sand." South Jersey sits atop a miles-thick layer of sand, not as fine as the Atlantic City beach sand of my childhood. But natural beach sand washes away, and that is disastrous for tourism, forcing beach towns to buy new sand from the inland sand mines, called sandwashes, which supply the thousands of truckloads needed for cement construction and beach repair.

And he showed us rocks, when there were any rocks. Living in New England, where every square yard of ground either displays large rocks or only shallowly conceals them, I can forget how few rocks we had, mostly an orange sandstone, which when tapped with the hammer showed deep veins of reddish purple. This was iron ore, bog iron, not very rich in metal but in the colonial period it was all there was available. In the Pine Barrens there's a museum of the old ironworks which made cannon balls for the Revolution.

On we went. Nature was all around: low blueberry bushes and poison ivy, bird nests and mushrooms, holly and mistletoe – where else can you see mistletoe in July?

And then we turned around and went home, presumably following the trail of wounded trees, dripping clear beads of sap from their sudden wounds.

After that day, I thought of myself as a hiker, a lover of the outdoors, a blazer of trails, a knower of nature's mysteries. Again and again, by myself and unprompted, I would hunt down a sassafras tree, count its four kinds of leaves, and grub in the ground nearby until I could find a candy-scented root to peel. I became a Boy Scout, earned the hiking merit badge, and even hiked around the Sangre de Cristo Mountains at Scouting's Philmont ranch.

At any point, if asked why I did all that, I would have said that my dad always took us for hikes in the woods. But it wouldn't have been true. That hike I just told you about, I am now certain, was the only one of its kind, ever. For whatever reason, it never happened again.

But it happened and I never forgot.

So take your kids outside. Don't feel inadequate if you can't do it every weekend or all summer, if you aren't a peak-bagging, high-pointing mountaineer, or a life-listing birder. Just haul them outside and take a hike. Once, just once, that might be enough.

Tamara Dean

Tamara Dean's stories and essays have appeared in The American Scholar, Creative Nonfiction, New Ohio Review, Orion, *and elsewhere. She holds an MFA from Vermont College of Fine Arts and is also the author of college textbooks on computer networking and* The Human-Powered Home, *a book about pedal-powered and hand-cranked devices.*

PERPETUAL OUTSIDER

A few years ago, I rode my bike through a pack of wolves.

Don't go into the wilderness alone. Especially if you're female.

I had rented a cabin near Grand Portage, Minnesota, for a week to write and hike and bike, alone. The last outpost on Lake Superior before Canada, Grand Portage blends the 21st and 18th centuries: a bright, timber-frame convenience store, gas station, casino, and lodge, all a short walk away from a reconstructed fur trading depot. The surrounding land—a slice of shore and the 1700-foot-high Sawtooth Mountain Range overlooking the lake—is owned by the Grand Portage Band of Lake Superior Chippewa and is mostly wild. I parked at the gas station mid-afternoon and unfolded my recumbent bike from the car's trunk. The 23-mile loop, recommended in a guidebook I found in Duluth, would take me down the coastal highway, up a small mountain, west along its crest, then down the mountain and back to the highway.

The ascent lasted five miles with no plateaus and some stretches rising at a 9% grade. But because I was alone and had the road to myself I could cycle at a leisurely pace. My recumbent, as comfortable as a recliner on wheels, put me at eye's level with the purple asters and deep under the shadowing pines.

"About a half mile past Speckled Trout Road... you will coast back to the Scenic Highway 61."

Once, the road had been paved. But for years, the elements had worked at returning it to wilderness. The pavement was cracked, pocked, rippled, patched where its flanks had fallen away, and swathed in gravel. Grass grew tall in the cracks. As soon as I started downhill, the bike bounced violently and rattled my spine. Coasting was impossible. I squeezed the brakes throughout the precarious descent, my pace about as slow as it was on the uphill climb.

Halfway down the mountain a white van, the only vehicle I'd seen during my outing, approached me from behind, and because conditions didn't allow us to share a lane, I pulled over and waved on the older couple inside. They waved back and crept by. Not long after they were out of sight I came upon them again, their van stopped in the middle of the road. Maybe they had broken down, I thought. Maybe they wanted to warn me of a washout ahead.

Be wary of strangers.

As I neared, I saw a four-legged figure in ahead and to the right of the van. The low evening sun beamed toward me, so the creature's only color was shadow. Another shape stepped onto the road. A third stood near the shoulder. My mind spun through the possibilities—fawn, moose calf, dog, no, coyote.

I stopped about twenty feet behind the van. The driver got out and walked toward me. "There's a pack of wolves in the road here," he said.

"I see."

Silence followed as I squinted and counted five shapes. Lean, dark, slow. Occasionally they glanced at us, but they acted unfazed, as if they didn't know a vehicle from a tree or this road from a forest path. Before then, the only wolves I'd seen were stuffed and posed in exhibits. I had expected live wolves to be elusive, suspicious, and threatening, but these animals appeared to be none of those things.

The man said, "I don't know how they might look at you, being so low to the ground…" They weren't pups, but given their size he guessed they were a young pack, which meant the mother couldn't be far away, and she wouldn't be too happy… His sentences kept trailing off, leaving me to fill in his fearful conclusions.

Wolves will do anything to avoid people.

While the pack loitered the man and I debated a solution. We decided that I would stay on my bike and ride next to his van so that we would become, effectively, one giant, imposing machine. I pulled up to my starting position on his left, then we advanced together slowly. The wolves moseyed north or south, but they didn't run. Nor did they lunge, glare, howl, or snarl. Cycling by them, I saw that they were charcoal gray, darker than I had expected. They remained placid and curious, sniffing and scanning as we passed. My legs pedaled, but the rest of me was taut with awareness, with the realization, *This is happening*.

Then the wolves were behind us. Like a meteor's flight, our traverse had been brilliant and quick, and we had no photos to prove what was now only a memory. The man and I stayed together for another quarter mile down the bone-jarring road, but we didn't speak of what we'd experienced. Finally he asked me if I knew my way back to Grand Portage, and once satisfied that I did, left me behind.

That night I told my story to the owner of the cabin I was renting. I saw that he didn't believe it, though he pretended to. His skepticism shouldn't have surprised me. So much about my wolf encounter contradicted conventional wisdom. The unexpected truths were: I was safe while alone in the wilderness, I could not coast downhill on that paved road, strangers proved to be trustworthy and helpful, the wolves didn't try to avoid us, and most surprising, the wolves were not at all threatening.

*   *   *

In a life of exploring the outdoors, and especially while living in a remote rural area for the past seven years, I have encountered so many contradictions to conventional wisdom that I'm obliged to question it. *Cougars don't live in southern Wisconsin.* But I have heard one roaring warnings from the woods behind our house, perhaps the same cat a neighbor saw while hunting. *Coyotes don't hunt full-grown deer.* But twice I have watched them do just that, prey and predator sprinting across my path, blind to me. *Don't argue with bears.* But I did, and won, to keep my backpack with its week's worth of food. Given such experiences, I would like to say that I'm immune to conventional wisdom, that I encounter nature free of assumptions. But the fact that I was stunned by the sight of the wolves, and then by their gentleness, proves otherwise.

The Western imagination has been trained to regard wolves as ferocious and rapacious. In Medieval bestiaries, wolves represented greed, avarice, and unchecked passion. They stood as models for etchings of the devil. In fairy tales, girls who strayed into the forest alone met their deaths when they met wolves. With such myths in their imaginations, Europeans who settled in America shot any wolves they saw and lured the others with poisoned bait. By the middle of the 20th century, only a few hundred of the estimated original population of two million animals remained in the lower 48 states. In 1974, according to the U.S. Fish and Wildlife Service, the only place you might have encountered a gray wolf was in northeastern Minnesota, where I had bicycled by them.

Wolves were protected in the 1960s under policies that predated the Endangered Species Act of 1973 and then under that provision. Their numbers began to rise. Now, approximately 6,000 gray wolves live in a fraction of their original U.S. range. But attitudes haven't changed much. Many Americans still regard wolves as predators so voracious that they threaten to decimate deer herds and pens full of livestock, to eat the family dog and maybe even the family itself, even though wolf attacks on humans are extremely rare.

In *Wild Echoes: Encounters With the Most Dangerous Animals in North America*, Charles Bergman proposes that the terror wolves invoke represents a denial of deep, personal urges. "The wolf in our imagination describes an interior landscape of fearful and alien impulses, projected onto the beast beyond." He claims that until we acknowledge the wolves' power in our imagination, we will continue to misunderstand the animals and threaten their existence. "More is at stake in saving a wild wolf than we realize. We need to save both the literal and the symbolic creatures. Part of the reason that so many animals are endangered, in this rational and empirical age, is precisely that we have forgotten the two faces of every creature. We have forgotten what animals *mean*."

Maybe people would not kill wolves if they confronted the creatures' role in their subconscious and, rather than trying to eliminate the object representing their fears, recognized that the fear is their own fabrication. But it's not enough to acknowledge the power of those cultural images. We would benefit ourselves and animals more if we replaced those images with more accurate and meaningful ones. The best possibility for doing this arises in the pursuit of direct experience—on a path in the woods, in a meadow, on a mountain pass.

Direct experience, rejecting conventions in favor of trusting one's own senses—this is what the Romantics, including Blake and

Wordsworth, advised. They were rebelling against the 18th century's push of Enlightenment, which they felt reduced the world, including nature, to scientific abstraction. Neil Evernden writes in his book, *The Natural Alien*, "The Romantic is a constant beginner in life, always learning, never content to be instructed by others." He quotes Robert Combs's *Vision of the Voyage*: "Unquestioned beliefs are the real authorities of a culture. Therefore, if an individual can express what is undeniably real for him, without invoking any authority beyond his own experience, he is transcending the belief systems of his culture."

What do we miss by relying on abstractions rather than our own senses? Abstractions, whether scientific or mythical (wolves are ferocious predators), lead to predictions (wolves will endanger anyone who gets close) that lead to reactions (wolves must be exterminated). By accepting abstractions not only do we harm unnecessarily, but we also miss an opportunity for wonder and understanding. Evernden contends that, "in turning to personal experience one foregoes the security of an established belief system with which to make sense of the world and exposes oneself to whatever comes. It means becoming a perpetual outsider. The gain for the individual is experience itself and the continual surprise of existence." Sustaining the continual surprise of existence, approaching the world as a perpetual outsider, we allow nature new meanings.

*   *   *

In 2012, wolves in the western Great Lakes region were removed from the federal Endangered Species List. That same year, Minnesota and Wisconsin introduced their first wolf hunting and trapping seasons since wolves were deemed a protected species. Minnesota's goal was to eliminate approximately 400 of its estimated population of about 3,000 wolves. Wisconsin aimed to eliminate no more than 201 of its 850 animals. Both states hailed the transition from wolf protection to wolf management as a sign of the wolf's success. And both cited the need to keep the wolf population in check (presumably, to preserve elk, moose, and deer herds) as one reason for the hunts, despite the fact that Minnesota's wolf population had remained stable in the fifteen years before hunting was allowed.

Although wolves are still considered elusive, some residents of northern Minnesota and Wisconsin *have* had direct experiences with them. To ranchers who have watched the wolves jump electric fences and take down cattle or sheep, the wolves are pests or even financial liabilities. Even so, a rancher in northern Wisconsin told reporters that he still considers a wolf sighting rare and wondrous. Hunters might agree with one honest man who wrote in an outdoor journal in that he doesn't hunt Minnesota's wolves to help keep the population in check or to bag a hide he can sell for a few hundred dollars on eBay or make into a rug. Nor, of course, will he eat the meat. "I see the wolf as the ultimate challenge," he said, revealing an age-old quest to conquer a ravenous beast, whether or not he acknowledges his projection of the same urges within.

Besides controlling the wolf population, the Wisconsin Department of Natural Resources (DNR) identified another goal for their new hunting and trapping season: to increase peoples' tolerance of wolves. Apparently, officials thought that if wolf-country residents knew the animals were prey as well as predator, they would feel less antipathy. The DNR was surprised when, according to a 2013 survey, the hunt did not increase anyone's tolerance. The idea of hunting—an abstraction that complements the myth of wolves as fearsome creatures—did nothing to counter either cultural or personal meanings for those residents.

Beyond Western imaginations, wolves do not necessarily evoke such fear. In the myths of the Chippewa (or Ojibwe) Indians of Minnesota, wolves were designed by the Creator to lead lives in parallel to humans. Clan-based, cooperative, intelligent, self-sacrificing, and nurturing are some of the qualities the two species are believed to share. Further, the Creator told the Chippewa that although they take different paths, what is done to the wolf will be done to the people. So tribes in Minnesota, including the Grand Portage Band of Lake Superior Chippewa, have prohibited hunting or trapping of wolves on their lands, except in rare instances of ceremony or self-defense. In the Grand Portage Band's territory of 56,000 acres in the Sawtooth Mountains, the pack I cycled through is probably safe from hunters.

In memory, my encounter with the wolves remains as Edward Abbey, in his book *Down the River*, described facing a mountain lion: "Mutual curiosity: I felt more wonder than fear." Since bicycling through the young pack, I hold an image of wolves as placid, curious, and self-assured. And that's just how I'd like to conduct myself in nature. To do so is to open to experience and not content myself with the instruction of others. It means going outside again and again—becoming, literally and symbolically, an outsider—to find out what's true.

Becky Lentz

Becky Lentz is a proud native of Michigan and Ann Arbor townie. This explains why the wolverine (Go Blue!) is her favorite animal. As a child growing up and still today there is no place that feels more like home to her than the shores of Lake Michigan. She enjoys writing, gardening and fishing. Becky worked with the National Wildlife Federation for over 20 years working to protect the Great Lakes and connect people to nature and wildlife.

WATCHING THE EAGLE FLY

I tell my son often that 90% of showing you care, whether about someone or something, is simply showing up. I believe NWF's Wildlife Nation™, holds that same promise of purposefully demonstrating both our love for nature and our families. My recent trip with my teenage son to see an eagle fly reinforced for me that spending time connecting with nature brings a vibrant clarity to what is most important to each of us.

On the night before I see the eagle fly, her trainer, Francie Krawcke, tells me the bird is having difficulty flying. It is breeding season and parts of her body are heavy and flying is uncomfortable. "She's moody," she adds. This seasonal and higher reproductive hormone change in the eagle triggers nesting behavior that includes becoming territorial to protect her nest, eggs, young and hunting grounds.

The next morning I write two notes, one to my son's school excusing him fifteen minutes early so he can see the eagle fly and one to my boss to ask if I can miss an afternoon management meeting so I can see the eagle fly. I feel a twinge of guilt and think of one of my favorite authors, poet and philosopher, Mark Nepo who says:

"Much of our anxiety and inner turmoil comes from living in a global culture whose values drive us from the essence of what matters. At the heart of this is the conflict between the outer definitions of success and the inner value of peace. We are encouraged, even trained to get attention when the renewing secret of life is to give attention."

This quote helps me remember why I choose to spend time with an eagle and my 13-year-old son Max rather than one more hour at work.

In the car on the way to the Leslie Science and Nature Center (LSNC), I watch out of the corner of my eye as my son's head moves up and down to the beat of his iPod. Earlier Max casually mentioned that he was going to bring his iPod "in case I get bored with seeing the eagle fly." When we arrive at the Leslie Science and Nature Center, I am more than happy to leave my Blackberry and Max's iPod in the car.

As we approach the eagle enclosure, she screeches repeatedly. "She wants to fly. She knows what's coming," I whisper to Max. A handful of other people are milling around waiting to see the eagle fly too. We're told by the LSNC staff that the eagle was pushed out of her nest when she was young and hurt her wing. Put in rehab, she imprinted, forgot she was an eagle, in other words. This eagle relates more to humans than other eagles and at five years old hasn't learned all the instincts she would have if raised in the wild, including how to fly. "She forgot who she is." My voice cracks. I feel teenage eyes giving me a warning look.

We traipse down the hill to where the eagle will practice flying between two wooden sawhorses about 50 feet apart. A rope, called a creance line, extends between the sawhorses and the eagle is fastened to it by a metal swivel attached to the Jesses (leather) that are attached

30

to the eagle's ankles. This set-up allows the eagle to travel the rope during her flight training.

We watch the eagle fly.

After awhile, someone in the small group gathered in the field shouts, "Can she go off the rope?" "She's ready," Francie answers, "But I am not." Francie's hand briefly stops at her heart and then she points at her head. "It's here. It's me. I'm not ready," she says. I glance at my growing boy. This boy, who stands in front of me every so often, looking right into my eyes saying, "I am almost as tall as you." To which I always give the same response, "It won't be long until I have to look up at you."

In this moment, I want more than anything to see the eagle off the creance line. I look up and in my mind's eye the eagle soars above my head, its mighty wings spread against the crisp blue sky.

Kiley Pratt

Kiley is a high school senior currently traveling and studying in Nepal. She is a soccer player, an artist, a musician, an outdoorswoman, and a voracious reader. Her home turf is New Haven, Vermont.

LABRADOR

Last summer, I spent six weeks in Labrador, Newfoundland, Canada, on the Section 2 canoe trip from Keewaydin Canoe Camps. For six weeks, six other girls, three staff members and I canoed our way through lakes and rivers, portaging whenever we came to land, bushwhacking our campsites, and generally trying to enjoy being in a place where not many people had ever been before. We began in Labrador City and went all the way to Lake Meneheck, where we caught the train to take us home. When I viewed the website, it sounded like an exciting outdoorsy adventure; when I first arrived, however, I was completely out of my comfort zone and utterly miserable.

We would paddle around 40 kilometers a day. During a normal day we also did lining, which involved pulling a canoe up rapids that were too swift to paddle. If an area was too shallow we would have to unload and pull the canoe over the rocks, then reload on the other side. But all of this was preferable to the dreaded portage, which involved carrying all of our gear over land to the next available body of water. The 'traditional Keewaydin way', taught to the first Keewaydin canoers by their First Nation guides, was to place a leather strap across your forehead, which was connected to whatever you were trying to carry, which would then rest on your back. The result of this was around 30-60 pounds of pressure that was mostly carried on your neck over almost two kilometers of land. I was not particularly fond of this carrying method, and found myself cursing all this tradition that kept us from using backpacks, or at least some method that had originated after 1900. The food was packed into boxes called 'wannigans', which were made of wood, had names painted on the side, weighed about 60 pounds each. We each had our own; mine was called 'White Fang', and although at first I hated White Fang with a passion, I developed a grudging affection towards it by the end of the trip. Because the wannigan would dig into my back during these portages, a scar developed that was fondly known as 'wannigan bite' by my fellow section mates and which made lying on my back, as well as portaging, extremely painful.

Labrador is not known for its sunny weather; in fact, I would guess we had less than five days on the trip where it did not rain. Most days it poured, drenching us as well as our gear. The famous Labrador blackflies were also prominent, making us all appear to be stricken with a severe case of the chicken pox. Any patch of skin left exposed would be quickly covered with the tiny black bugs, and an entire blackfly homicide had to be conducted inside the tent before sleeping. Even then, you would sometimes awake to an area of skin swollen with bites that had not been there the night before.

At this point, you may be asking yourself why anyone would wish to submit themselves to this kind of adventure, something I wondered myself many times during those six weeks. But when I had pushed myself to the very edge of my abilities, when I would wake up in the morning and know as soon as I got out of bed I would get pushed to my body's physical limit, those days were when I had some of the most beautiful, bizarre and indescribable moments of my life.

One of the most amazing parts about being in Labrador was the wildness of it. I, like many teenagers my age, spend most of my days in contact with many different people, technology, and developed areas. On this trip, there was nothing developed about the places we visited.

The only kind of technology we had any contact with was the plane that brought us our food three weeks in, and the train we caught to take us home. The only people I saw all six weeks were my section mates and the driver of the floatplane. The paths we took were not marked, and were mostly made by our staff thirty minutes before we portaged over them. I had never been in a place that was so untouched by humans, and it amazed me that 'the wild' of my childhood books set in the 1700's was still around, in some ways, today. Even though the scenery around us was often cloaked in mist or rainclouds, there were still many moments that I got a sudden shock at being in a place that was so incredibly unlike anything I knew. It was beautiful to me, all that wilderness. There were little places I remember vividly. I remember going back to find a hat I had dropped on a portage. It was an overcast day, but the rain hadn't started to fall yet. There was a river running along the path, with rocky banks and white caribou moss on the outside of it. The whole trip there was nothing but caribou moss underfoot, which made it seem as though snow had fallen thick between the pine trees. And in the midst of all this white was a tiny patch of green moss surrounding a flat rock next to a small river. I stopped searching for my hat and walked over to sit on the rock. The wind blew in the trees and the birds were quiet in the distance, and the river babbled softly on its way to the next lake. The sun came out from behind the clouds and lit the peaks of the tiny waves in the river, sending tiny diamonds sparkling down the stream. Perhaps five people, I guessed, had seen this place and taken the time to stop and look at it. A tiny spot in this vast wilderness. I felt so big and so small at the same time. I knew that when I left, the river would keep sparkling and the wind would keep blowing and the moss would be just as white as before. All of these things would remain, but I was just passing through. I had many philosophical moments like this one on that trip; I mean, it was kind of hard not to when you have many hours on the water and on the land portaging and you need things to occupy your mind. Sometimes I would talk to my section mates while paddling, and many Dixie Chicks songs were sung, but more often than not we were silent. I discovered a lot about myself during that six-week trip. I was pushed to my limit again and again, and so many times I thought, 'This is it. I'm done.' Apparently I wasn't done, because the next day I would get up and do it all over again.

I wondered a lot why I was doing this, and why I kept going. I sure wasn't doing it for the bug bites and the bruises and the scratches, nor did I have any illusion that this was somehow going to make me a pro canoe woman with biceps the size of desk lamps. I guess I was doing it for my section mates, so as not to hold them back and try and create a good environment for all of us, but as much as I didn't want to disappoint them I don't think that alone would have forced me to rise from my warm sleeping bag every morning and brave the rain. I did it for myself, for those little moments when I was on a portage and sweating so hard and crying and I would tell myself, 'I'm just going to fall down right here and never get up,' yet I still put one foot in front of the other and made it to the end. For the moments sitting on a rocky beach eating GORP and talking about red velvet cake with my section mates, and laughing at our ridiculous appearance and the number of red dots peppering our skin. For the moments when the sun would come out and we would all stop paddling and I would take off my wet clothes and lay them on the wannigans to dry, then resume paddling with the feeling of sun on my back. For nights around the fire, scraping the remains of a charred cookie that hadn't turned out to be edible. For our clubbing night, where we broke out all the spandex we had and ate absurd amounts of corn. For the moments when I realized how much farther I could go, how much more faith I had in myself, and how much I could persevere. For the moments in the tent at night. When it's quiet, and the sun has already set and I've just pulled on my sleeping clothes and pulled off my wet socks and climbed into my sleeping bag. It's chilly outside, but inside the sleeping bag it is the most comfortable thing in the world. For the moment when I'm almost asleep, when I have a whole eight hours until I have to do anything again. When a loon cries on the lake and I fall asleep with a smile on my face, because even though I'm three hours in a van, a ferry ride, a train ride, and countless days of paddling out in the middle of nowhere, I'm here. I'm safe and warm and content and no one else has gotten me to this point. I've made it.

Bill Dodge

Bill Dodge was last seen walking into a cloud on Silver Lake in Vermont. A former Montreal bookstore owner, art print gallery owner and book columnist, his photography is available at DodgeStudioArts.com

THE MAGIC OF THE OUTDOORS

Our first physical adventures in the outdoors are not always the most noble or flattering. As a young outcast in a family of seven children, I was a natural rebel and prone to all kinds of mischief. Let's just say that my parents' neighborhood was a bit over-sedated. Most of the folks living there were either retired, semi-retired or in transition to Florida. My younger sisters, being more open to persuasion and to acts of juvenile delinquency than my three older brothers, liked to join me in scaring these cranky grey-haired residents. We would lurk outside some neighbor's window and start imitating wolves, night owls, feral cats and other nocturnal wildlife. When it came to making a quick getaway - climbing up drainpipes and jumping off garage roofs were just a few of the required skills for our street gang. My sisters were surprisingly patient with me until the day I tricked them, on a dare, into taking off all their clothes and streaking down the sidewalk from our house to the street's main fire hydrant. I promised to do the same but only if they went first. I also promised, as a bonus, to throw in some naked cartwheels. Twenty seconds was all the time it took for me to toss their shirts, pants and underwear up into the neighbor's apple tree. My sisters all survived their first exposure to the elements. Of course, it didn't take long for them to devise their own sweet revenge.

On some deep instinctive level, I think the appeal of nature has always been associated, for me, with the wildness of the unknown and what is beyond our control. Whether listening to the wind during a storm's approach or staring up at the billions and billions of random stars littering the night sky, the mystery of consciousness has a way of keeping us all bewildered and spellbound. As a young and somewhat restless adventurer, the journey from snowball fights, cloud-gazing, kick-the-can, and outdoor hockey to a six-month job as an officer's messman on the Gypsum Empress and then a 9,000 kilometer trek on the Trans-Siberian and Trans-Mongolian Railroads, seems like a trail that was always calling out to me. The world was teeming with unexplored places and inexplicable forces.

Arriving in Vermont in the mid-nineties with my wife and two young children, I was aware of the Green Mountain State's reputation as a pristine playground for nature lovers. My wife's Danish-Canadian father and French Quebec mother had retired in Westford, VT, from Montreal. Their mostly-forested homestead, home to deer, coyotes, and hawks as well as bear poop, snake skins, beavers and wild turkeys, filled our kids' lives with wide-eyed wonder. As a young native of Massachusetts, my Dad had spent several summers working in a hut in the White Mountains of Maine and he sometimes spoke dismissively of Vermont. Compared to the White Mountains' Presidential Range, the Green Mountains were, in his unbiased view, mere hiccups. But when I first took in the full height and breadth of Mt. Mansfield, it looked pretty impressive to me.

My wife and I got our first taste of Vermont's outdoor life when we dipped our oars in the Lamoille River, shooting the very light rapids by the bridge in Jeffersonville. I remember this outing because of the surprising greeting we received from a fisherman who looked stranded on some rocks in the river. With his waders, fishing vest and floppy hat, he could have stepped out of an LLBean catalog. He looked way too well-outfitted to be a local but we both thought it was pretty cool that people actually hitched canoe rides in Vermont. This gentleman was headed downriver to Cambridge.

Since we were big city slickers from out of state, our immersion into Vermont's outdoor culture and the world famous slopes of Jay Peak owed a lot to savvy middle school kids. They were up on all the latest gear from Vermont's legendary Burton snowboard company. We also learned about the many hiking and biking opportunities across Vermont through our children's friends. Mount Elmore, Snake Mountain, Mount Hunger, Smuggler's Notch (Sterling Pond), Camel's Hump, Pleasant Valley Road, Greenbush Road...the must-do list, we soon learned, is always expanding. We found out that even the lowly Mount Philo, if you get off its paved road and onto a wooded path, can offer some exciting encounters with wildlife, mostly in the form of "extreme sports" enthusiasts who are capable of running over anything in the midst of a high-speed ascent.

While working as a journalist and bookstore owner in Montreal, I met a photographer who had built his own custom landscape camera so that he could capture the genius of the landscape architect, Frederick Law Olmsted. Olmsted's panoramic vistas still bring flocks of migrating birds and tourists to Vermont's Shelburne Farms every year. Olmsted believed that preserving vistas with an open view of the horizon was essential to human health and to restoring the right perspective of the "human scale" and our place in nature. A big walker and self-educated engineer, his landscape design at Shelburne Farms and many other famous green-spaces across America, continues to inspire people of all ages to walk outdoors.

Without a doubt, some of the most exalting places our family has visited are on Vermont's mountaintops. There is a sense of solace up there on The Long Trail, and a deep yearning to experience some permanence in the midst of the impermanent. As I reflect back on the days when my sisters and I were trying to rouse our neighbors from their sleep, I realize I'm becoming one of those slower and cranky elders now, scrambling to get out of the way of the next generation climbing the Green Mountains and aware of the growing cycles that are so much bigger than one life.

There is also a deep connection between the frontiers of nature and the frontiers of our imagination. Before I came across the landscape philosophy of Olmsted and long before my adventures on the high seas and distant railroads, there was a wilderness that I explored every night, a dreamworld filled with mysterious predators and forces of nature. The British novelist, Graham Greene, once wrote: "We are all immigrants from the country of childhood." It's in that first "great outdoors" - the country of our childhood imaginations - that we all learn about the magic of being alive. That was where I first learned how to fly. My take-offs were always at night and from the same spot on the downward slope of a hill in Murray Park. The final step off the ground into the air always happened in a full sprint and under a canopy of stars. I know I'm still open to more flying lessons.

William Luginbuhl

Born Des Moines, Iowa, 1929. Gardening commenced 1932 and continued until college graduation (B.S., 1949). Gardening interrupted during medical school (M.D., 1953) and residency training. Recommenced in U.S. Army (Capt.) 1957-59. Gained in intensity on moving to Vermont, 1959. Continued unabated since, although serving as Professor of Pathology and Dean of the Medical School at the University of Vermont until retirement in 1991 imposed some limits. Moved to a retirement community in Pennsylvania in 2011 where some gardening continues.

APPLES

In the fall of 1959 I was discharged from the Army Medical Corps. My wife, Vi, and I moved to Burlington, Vermont, where I had accepted a position at the Medical College of the University of Vermont. With the approach of winter we bought a small house on a small lot in Burlington. During the long winter I began to plan my garden, a hazardous undertaking. Planning a garden during the long, cold, snowy Vermont winter is like writing your grocery shopping list when you're starving.

At long last the spring came. I spaded up the small front lawn and replanted the grass. I dug up the very small south lawn and planted a vegetable garden. The backyard was somewhat larger and after very little thought, I decided I would grow apples, largely because it was something that I hadn't done before and thought it would be a learning experience. It certainly proved to be that.

41

In the spring I purchased seven semi-dwarf apple trees of seven different varieties. Over the next three summers they required a limited amount of care: mulching, fertilizing, watering, and spraying a few times. They grew quite well and even produced a few apples. I felt quite knowledgeable.

In the spring of the fourth year we sold the property and built a home in the country on five acres of former cow pasture. Because the apple trees were getting a bit crowded, I moved three of them to the new property before selling the old. Because those three small trees looked lonely on a five-acre lot, I purchase a half dozen more trees of additional varieties, all on semi-dwarf rootstock.

At this point I should explain that modern apple trees are actually composed of two different individuals: the roots are part of one individual and the tops are part of another, the named variety. The roots control the size of the tree. My initial trees were on an English rootstock called East Malling Seven. All are from pieces of root propagated from one original tree. The tops are all grown from another individual. For example, all Red Delicious apples are propagated from a seedling tree discovered in an Iowa barnyard by a Quaker farmer. The tops are grafted on the roots. This process first involves growing a small tree of the desired rootstock. Then in late summer when this little tree is a well developed small whip, a single bud of the desired variety is inserted under its bark just above ground level and allowed to heal in. The following spring the tree is cut off just above this inserted bud forcing the bud into growth of a new top now of the desired variety. Thus the top of an entire mature apple tree grows from a single small bud.

After planting these additional trees I had a small orchard of seemingly modest potential requiring modest labor. However, the next spring I met a university colleague from the College of Agriculture who was in charge of the apple research program, apple production being a major industry in Vermont. He was experimenting with a new apple rootstock called Malus Robusta. He had a number of these trees in which the bud graft had failed. He offered these to me and since my little orchard was under control, I decided to take ten of these trees. Since these trees were destined to become quite large and since I didn't want large quantities of a single variety, I decided to graft multiple varieties on each tree. This I did over the next several years grafting each limb of every tree to a different variety. This was done using a different grafting technique called whip grafting.

To whip graft one takes a short section of a small branch of the desired variety. This section is about the diameter of a lead pencil and contains two buds. Actually only one is needed but the second is a reserve in case the first fails to grow. This small section, called a scion, is carefully joined to the cut end of a branch of the same diameter that is part of the tree being grafted. The union of the scion and the branch is carefully wrapped with a strip of rubber and coated with a tar based grafting paint. This process is done in the early spring and, if all goes well, a new limb of the desired variety develops. After several years when all the grafting was completed, each of the ten Malus Robusta trees had eight or nine varieties for a total of about eighty-five varieties. Most of these were antique apples, varieties popular in the past. Finally in the spirit of adventure, I grafted twenty-eight varieties onto one semi-dwarf tree.

During these years I had also added a few more semi-dwarf trees so at this point I had over one hundred varieties of apples. During these same early years I discovered that I actually didn't know much about growing apples. They required pruning, fertilizing, mulching, spraying, thinning and harvesting at the appropriate time. With a hundred varieties, at least one was subject to every known apple disease. Every known apple insect pest found one or more varieties they particularly liked. Without wishing to engage in controversy, let me simply state that in my opinion it is impossible to successfully grow many different apple varieties in Vermont without spraying with a variety of legal agents. To do this, I had to acquire a pesticide license, which required study and passing an examination followed by continuing education. It also required larger equipment, a power driven sprayer and a tractor to pull it.

During these early years when things were still under control, I met another university colleague from Agriculture, an entomologist. He suggested that I keep bees to ensure pollination. I spent the next winter building a beehive and multiple frames for the bees to fill with brood: eggs and developing bees and other frames to fill with honey. In the spring I ordered a package of bees by mail. They came in a small wooden partially screened box, a half pound or so of worker bees and a queen in a small cage. A few days later my wife received a phone call from our rural mail carrier. The bees had arrived but the screen was torn and the bees were crawling all over the outside of the box. He wouldn't put them in his car to deliver them so we had to pick them up. Since I was tied up at the office that meant Vi, who indeed picked them up. It pays to marry a farm girl. That night reading the directions, I installed them in the hive.

There was one other adventure with the bees. Bees multiply by swarming. A strong hive will raise a second queen and when she is mature, the old queen and a large number of bees leave the old hive and look for a new home. Initially they land near the old hive, clustered in a large ball. Scouts are sent out to search for a new home and when one is found the swarm flies to it. One evening as Vi and I were leaving for a dinner party I spied a swarm of bees in one of my trees. Fortunately I had an empty hive available, so I quickly put on my protective bee veil, grabbed the smoker, and captured the swarm. Meanwhile Vi called our hostess to explain why we would be late. I'm not sure the hostess believed her.

The beekeeping was quite successful. The bees pollinated the apples and produced lots of honey. They also produced swarms of bees so we soon had three hives, which Vi established as the upper limit. The bees required care during the season and in the fall the extra honey, a couple hundred pounds, had to be extracted. This involves using smoke to drive the bees off the honeycomb-filled frames and bringing them in for extracting. For this process we used a hand-cranked centrifuge. Initially we did this in the kitchen, but the honey had a tendency to fly about and coat various surfaces. Vi limited extraction to the garage. Unfortunately, there a few bees always found a way in, attempting to retrieve their honey.

Over the years the apple trees got bigger, the bees kept busy, and apple production increased alarmingly. The first apples were ready in early August and from then until November multiple varieties were ripe for picking each week. Some of the older varieties do not bear every year so we usually produced seventy-five or eighty varieties. What to do with the apples became a problem.

I solved this problem happily. Each day I put one or more bushels in my truck and drove to the medical college. I left them in the student lounge with a card giving the name of the variety and a short history of the apple. At the end of the day the baskets were always empty. An additional benefit was that some students liked to come on weekends and help with the harvest.

Sometimes there was another problem. If a hard freeze was predicted, all the remaining apples needed to be picked. Often this involved picking after dark using the truck lights. Several years this occurred when I was out of town, leaving the task to Vi.

Finally there was one other apple adventure. Our youngest son ate a Red Delicious apple and found eight seeds which he wanted to plant. I explained that apples don't come true from seed, that all eight would be different and none were likely to be good. Nevertheless we planted them and grew eight little trees. Not wanting to wait years to learn their value, I took wood from each and grafted it into an older bearing tree. After several years each began to produce. All were fairly good apples but one was exceptional. A large yellow apple with a beautiful red cheek, it was tender and very juicy with superb flavor. It had one fault, however. It was too tender for modern apple processing methods.

As a further learning experience, I decided to obtain a plant patent. Part of the learning experience was discovering that patent attorneys are very expensive. But in due course a patent was obtained and the apple is officially Vermont Gold. Over the years I produced by grafting several hundred Vermont Gold trees for a friend who is a commercial grower. He now receives a premium price for them.

Eventually the time came for me to retire so I lost my student consumers. It was also harder to get out of bed at 4:30 or 5:00 a.m. to care for apples and my back no longer appreciated lifting eighty-pound hive bodies full of honey. There was only one solution. We sold our home and orchard to a younger couple and built a new home on Lake Champlain. There I started grafting pears.

What did I learn from all my apple growing? Three things: first, newer varieties of apples are better than the old; second, childhood memories of wonderful old apple varieties are mostly nostalgia; third, hungry medical students will eat any variety of free apples.

One final comment: my wife, Vi, is very fond of apples, but I don't particularly care for them.

Tessa Fancher

Born and raised in Vermont, Tessa now lives in Monterey, California where she spends her time working toward a double masters (International Education Management and Public Administration) and exploring the beaches, redwoods, and deserts of California. In her "free time" she can most likely be found dreaming of (and sometimes traveling to) foreign cities, mountains and islands.

MOUNTAINS TO CLIMB

Yesterday, while hiking Mount Mansfield, my boyfriend and I fell into a familiar conversation: How are we going to get really rich, really fast? In a lot of ways this is just our way of talking about current events, technology, philosophy and the future of the world. Yesterday, on a beautifully warm fall day in VT, I was using our ongoing question to bring up an article I had recently read about technology addiction. My idea had been to convert my family's secluded lake house into a sanctuary where city dwellers plagued with technology addictions could de-stress. The luxury of being denied WIFI and 4G would cost them a large sum thus making us really rich, really fast. I was joking, but as we discussed the logistics I realized how lucky I have been to grow up in Vermont where we don't need to resort to such extremes, the outdoors isn't something to seek out, it is a simple reality of life.

I am at a loss when I try to put into words what nature means to me. It is a deeply engrained part of my life; it has always been available to me as a playground, a classroom and a means to escape. Summers, winters, days off from work, vacations and subsequently the person I have become has been defined by my access to nature.

I recently read that the average American checks their phone 150 times per day! While shocking, there is no denying I am one of the Americans driving that average up. The difference is I know better. I know to turn to nature when I am stressed or upset, not my computer or TV. I know that there is comfort in a familiar hike through the woods or a running path by the lake. I know this remedy is free and extremely effective and I also know if I spend too much time staring at my phone I'll turn into a mindless and un-ambitious blob—or worse.

Recently I was traveling alone in a foreign city. I was unfamiliar with the geography, customs and people of the city—and a lot less familiar with the language than I pretended to be. After paying 20X what a local would for a cab ride from the airport to my hostel I felt uncertain of myself and my decision to travel to Peru alone. Once safely in my hostel I spent about five minutes staring at my cell phone and wishing for the comfort and familiarity of a functioning phone with my friends and family just a text away. Luckily, I was raised to find comfort in the outdoors. Motivated purely by instinct, I walked out of my room and out of the hostel. Instead of heading into town, towards the city, I walked the other direction towards the mountains that surrounded the city. I was sleep deprived and pretty sure the whole trip was a mistake. I pushed that thought out of my mind and focused on finding the base of the mountain. Soon I was on the mountain and only able to focus on breathing and wiping sweat out of my eyes. After several hours I reached the top—there had been no one with me on the road or the trail but surprisingly there were quite a few people at the top. The summit was incredible, there were ruins of an ancient city scattered around—sans signs and fences to keep the public off—in fact, there were children and llamas alike climbing all over the weathered stones. I weaved through the abandoned shelters towards a large religious statue built at the top of the mountain, which overlooks the city. There I sat and from my seat among the ruins, looked down on the modern city of Cusco.

At the time I didn't feel fear, just gratitude—I felt grateful I had been brave enough to take this trip, grateful for the weather, the view and the other people quietly looking down at the city. Now looking back I'm grateful for the love of nature which has built up inside me without me even realizing it. I am grateful that my instinct was to look for comfort in a foreign city the same way I do at home—by hiking outdoors. That one hike on the afternoon I arrived, dictated the mood for the rest of the trip. I had a goal, to hike more of the surrounding mountains, and a new confidence which comes from a fresh challenge.

When I left, just over a week later, I had hiked multiple Peruvian mountains and felt I had an excellent understanding of the country's geography, fauna and wildlife. Seeking out comforts and similarities in nature allowed me to meet wonderful locals I never would have met, improve my Spanish and find a meditative calm within myself. It would have been equally as brave to travel to Peru alone and spend my week sitting in cafes, looking up what my friends were up to on Facebook and drinking cafe con leche. I feel I have a deeper understanding of the country and myself by unconnecting and finding comfort outdoors.

As I think back on our conversation yesterday, it seems less like a joke. Everyone should see nature as an outlet, a resource and a friend when everyday life seems too overwhelming. In this way you can travel the world, experience incredible things and always know there is the comfort of the ocean, a hiking trail or a bike path nearby.

Greg Seitz

Greg Seitz is a writer, outdoorsman and communications consultant. He is the editor of St. Croix 360, a news and stewardship website dedicated to the St. Croix River watershed. Greg works with several nonprofit partners in the region to engage the public in conservation, the arts and community development. He previously worked on behalf of the nation's most popular wilderness area, the Boundary Waters in northern Minnesota, and continues to write and develop communications strategy focused on the region for the Quetico-Superior Foundation. Greg is also a contributing editor for Minnesota Trails magazine. He lives in Minnesota with his wife Katie, daughter Annika, and black lab Lola. His website is www.gregseitz.com.

ROOKERY ROOTS

The town where I grew up has the Twin Cities on one side and a wild river on the other. Stillwater, Minnesota, is on the banks of the St. Croix River; its name is taken from where it sits at the head of the slow-moving final 20 miles of the river before it joins the Mississippi. Just a little ways upstream is a broad valley of islands and bluffs, an area of beauty and silence which I first encountered when I was seventeen years old.

In high school, I skied (slowly) on the cross-country ski team, I was the co-editor of the newspaper, and I was a member of the Bio-Earth Club, which was led by former Arctic canoe guide Jeff Ranta. It was with Mr. Ranta that a group of club members paddled down the St. Croix one spring afternoon, seeking a Great Blue Heron rookery, which

I would learn is not only remote but is also like visiting the time of the dinosaurs.

We went one afternoon in the spring, the floodplain forest gray and flat. Only a few hundred yards after pushing away from the landing in our fleet of aluminum canoes, Mr. Ranta led most of us into a narrow side channel, nearly invisible from far across the river because it formed an s-curve, appearing as one wooded wall. He led "most of us" because a couple canoes got out too far ahead and paddled past the turn out of earshot and only finally looked back and saw us waiting for them, waving arms. We sat and watched while they fought their way back up against the current.

Entering the backwater, everything was quiet, except for the birds. It was not very leafy yet, but the banks sang in stereo. Such a springtime chorus is a chaotic melody of joy and hope and it has come forth from the banks every spring for millennia. Who knows if a bunch of high school kids heard any of it?

After a few miles of frog and bird and teenager song, the Stillwater Area High School Bio-Earth Club arrived at the rookery.

Visiting a heron rookery is, I imagine, much like canoeing back in time 100 million years. The water was up high enough we could paddle right across the island below the nests, winding through the maples and cottonwoods and willows and ash. Above our heads, the birds flopped and squawked. With five-foot wingspans and long spindly legs, they are made for flight and wading in shallow waters, but not particularly for perching.

Entering the noisy rookery shut us right up. It always does. We drifted below, intruders in a world most of us didn't know existed. We saw with our own eyes that not only does it exist, this ancient island was only 20 miles from our school. The valley there is particularly broad, more than a mile from bluff to bluff. Paddling through such an expanse always feels far from the world of concrete and steel, highways and politics, television and automobiles – and from people who don't know such places.

We drifted speechless through the rookery, and then down a couple more miles of river. We weren't quite so raucous the rest of the way. We were off the river by dark, home to do school work. Then back to the newspaper and friends and being young. But I have gone back. I've begun to get to know that piece of river, learning its spring-fed creeks, campsites, sandbars – even individual trees and rocks and bird nests.

And with my wife Katie and friends and strangers and dogs, we have explored the reach of the St. Croix and its tributaries. The exploration will be a lifetime project, one of our most important endeavors.

***

Many springs, the rookery stretch of the St. Croix is our first paddling destination. It's the closest piece of good water, and the herons never cease to awe. The channel we accessed the rookery from that first trip was plugged by a huge snag maybe 10 years ago and is impassable now. Channels are as fluid as water itself – getting to know a river is about watching it change.

On such spring trips, ducks regularly explode out from along the banks, making a big commotion, trying to distract us from their nests. We call it the "Annual Spring Waterfowl Harassment Tour." A traditional trip that started with simply wanting to wet a paddle after the long winter has become about birdsong and breeding and the people who want to paddle cold gray days in April.

The St. Croix's watershed has become the most significant geographical boundary of my world, more important than city or county or state. It defines an area nearly as big as New Jersey, most of it sharing a familiar landscape of rivers and lakes, and more deer than people.

Last spring, I paddled 92 miles of the St. Croix's largest tributary, the Namekagon – nearly the whole river. A group of friends also organized a second annual upper river Fourth of July weekend flotilla, with a big crew and 12 miles amidst cedars and rock and rushing water. I've paddled in the Snake River Canoe Race two years, which happens in early May and runs 14 miles of the river above Mora, Minnesota.

Seeking to get to know the river better, I've netted shocked fish with Department of Natural Resources employees, waded remote beaver ponds with researchers looking for trout, fished for smallmouth bass, floated under the moon and to the song of sandhill cranes. We have paddled in the rain and in the sun, swam at a blur of beaches, hiked along the bluffs and the banks.

And yet there is more.

The river is big and broad and carries a lot of water at Stillwater. It is as much lake as river the rest of the way. Big boats run over its surface, and it has lots of beauty, not many houses, and a few good beaches. Down here there are parks and nature centers that have preserved a little of the old valley as the city bleeds east. Bison roam native prairie not a mile south of I-94, slipping through tall grasses like ghosts. At one park, there is a big sandbar where a creek spills into the river, a short hike down the bluff for swimming and sun.

There are holes in Lake St. Croix 90 feet deep and the river regularly moves 75,000 gallons of water every second where it meets the Mississippi at Prescott, Wisconsin. All that water comes from the north. The river gathers from 8,000 square miles of Minnesota and

Wisconsin, much of it forested or wet country. There are roughly 600 miles of "significant" streams which enter it above Stillwater; the U.S. Geological Survey counts 1,964 but not all of that is navigable. There are 1,920 miles the other direction, between Stillwater and the Gulf of Mexico via the Mississippi.

Perhaps the last people to live here before European contact are called the Oneota, and archaeologists are studying mounds and pottery shards almost a thousand years old, found on the river bank south of Marine on St. Croix. They were farmers who used finely crushed mussel shells from the river to strengthen their pottery. One pot found in Wisconsin could hold 15-20 gallons of liquid but the walls are just a third of an inch thick. In a city park on the bluff in Hudson, Wisconsin, centuries-old Dakota Indian burial mounds look over the broad river below, a view I would also choose for eternity.

***

Visitors to the St. Croix most often hear about its history the past 200 years. There were fur traders and explorers who traveled the region, and then the Europeans took the land and the river and its timber amidst conflict between the Ojibwe and the Dakota, and logged the great pine forests, millions of logs floating down the river every spring for decades.

It is this logging that I think about the most while on the river. One cool October day, I floated down the rookery stretch with an old friend named Ryan and his girlfriend Rachel, who was visiting the St. Croix for the first time. The herons were already gone south for the year, and water levels were low, so we stuck to the main channel.

We were a little pressed for time, but I added a couple more miles to our usual float, taking out at one of the river's most popular state parks. I think it was because Rachel had never been on the river before and I wanted to show her the limestone banks and tall white pines clinging to the rock on the section of river bordered by the park.

The St. Croix is a gorgeous river, but its beauty can be quiet and require time to get to know and love. Much of it flows through flat floodplain forests, the banks sandy or grassy, the trees homogeneous hardwoods. It is a wild river, with few houses in sight, and clean, clear water. But perhaps because it is so close to the Twin Cities, a rookie to the river would assume it is subjugated by man, that it is as densely populated as any of our tourist lakes, that its water is fouled by lawns, wastewater and farms. None of that is true, but I have found that sometimes people see what they expect, not what is true.

There are spots, though, which can grab the attention of a first-time visitor. This park is one of them. Green rock drops 10 feet into the water. A popular walking trail runs along the bank, screened by stands of mature pines, which grow directly up from the very edges of the drop-offs. From the path, those pines frame the river and the opposite shore perfectly, like windows.

The 2,200-acre park was created when the daughter of a lumber baron donated his holdings to the state. Men like him made their fortunes de-timbering the valley, but this park contains some of the prettiest pines along the river. They are noticeable especially in the fall when the deciduous trees turn red and orange and gold, and winters when the surrounding woods are brown and gray and muted. Then, the pines' color seems to take on a darker hue, and they are a feast for eyes hungry for the color of growth.

Because of how dry it had been all through late summer and early fall, meteorologists and arborists (nearly all Minnesotans) predicted a fast and disappointing autumn. The trees would turn brown and yellow and then the leaves would fall. We were wrong. It had been a beautiful, luxurious season.

As we paddled, we talked of what those old-growth pine forests must have been like. Think of trunks 12 feet across. Think of the forest floor covered in a thick carpet of soft red needles, muffling all sound. Think of the fallen trees, dead of old age, decaying into soil. Think of stretching your neck to look up toward the sky, those giants swaying in the wind 150 feet above. If I could travel through time just once, I think it might be to the St. Croix Valley 1,000 years ago. Think of the silence.

***

Fifteen years after graduating from Stillwater Area High School, I still ski a little, do a lot of writing, and still paddle the St. Croix. The place has formed me as a person, and it feels like my life is written on its landscape. My own stories mingle with the river's.

The first trip to the rookery not only led me back to that spot many times, but also all over the country drained by the river, and defined by it. There is something specific about this region that ties it together, something common I find wherever I go. It's the sense of being at home.

Jenny Montagne

Jenny Montagne is an artist, writer, and reluctant outdoorsperson. She is interested in how people exist in digital landscapes and people, in general. Jenny works for the Vermont Agency of Natural Resources and lives in Plainfield, Vermont, with her companion, Ryan, and two cat-children.

UNLEARNING BAD HABITS

I was a TV kid. I came home from school and watched hours of television before my dad came home and made dinner, during which I would watch the black and white TV in the kitchen or read books at the table. After dinner, I would do an hour or two of homework with the television blaring in the background and then settle into bed with my TV on low all night, the light flashing grey and blue on the wall as I slept.

I could easily recite quotes from all sorts of television shows. My equally screen-obsessed neighbors and I would play a game called "TV Tag" wherein, if you were in danger of being tagged, you could grant yourself immunity by screaming the name of a TV show and the channel it was broadcast on. My point of distinction was that after the age of seven, I didn't really like cartoons; I preferred the Nick-at-Nite circuit of reruns like *Growing Pains* and, my favorite, *A Different World*. The problem was that these shows played very early in the morning, beginning around 5:30 a.m., so naturally, I would wake up then and watch before school, often falling back asleep until 7:00 a.m., when everyone else started waking up.

I would guffaw when my friends said they had TV time limits, or worse, didn't have televisions at all. I thought it meant that their parents were restrictive weirdos, too new age and sterile. Worse was the fear that maybe my friends didn't want to watch television as much as I wanted to. Afternoons at friends' houses often amounted to homework before dinner, creative dance, the writing and subsequent acting of small parts in semi-improvised skits performed for an audience of each other. If things were fun, I would think how nice it was to unplug for a little while, and maybe feel the warm spark of human connection. But if the play date ended in an argument, I would long to just be home on the couch in front of the television.

As much as I remember my childhood as that of a television-obsessed zombie, I can also recall marked efforts on the part of my parents and grandparents to get outside and do something. The problem was that I would so often get bored outside, thinking of all of the other things I could be doing, or feeling forced to breathe fresh air and move around.

During the summer, my siblings and I would go on camping weekends, hikes, and picnics with my parents. My memories of these trips are fleeting images of trees and water, punctuated by the telling of horrifying campfire stories that still make me feel nervous to be in the woods at night.

I would often hang out in the forested area of the park at the end of my street, watching classmates go off of amateur BMX jumps, or swim in Lake Champlain with my sister, but this never felt like real time spent outdoors, doing anything of note – I was just trying to pass the time. Sometimes in the winter, I would force myself to go on long, cold walks in order to feel deep and poetic, most likely so that someone would see me and know that I was a great thinker, feeling things.

The summer after my mom died – when I was nine – my grandpa took my brothers and me on a camping trip to a remote state park in the northeast kingdom of Vermont. I remember canoeing out to a lone rock in the middle of a lake with a tree growing on it. It rained all week, but, maybe because I was so young, my memories are of the lush trees, our tents tucked cozily under a tarp, and a foot-shaped rock that I found with my grandpa, on which we wrote the date – August 5, 1997.

As I got older, I would occasionally take weekend trips to the mountain town that my dad was planning on moving us to. While we were there, we might go for a swim at the base of a natural waterfall. I was often distracted by other things like the water washing away my makeup to reveal my acne (of course I put on makeup to go hiking) and how I looked to the groups of boys jumping off of rocks into the water.

When we did move to the town of Bristol, only 45 minutes south of Burlington, I felt like I had been betrayed. In my old neighborhood – a phrase that would grow so tired and clichéd during the first months at my new school – I could walk everywhere, or ride my bike in a pinch. This was a driving town. In exchange for driving everywhere, residents were treated to overwhelming views of mountains, long stretches of corn growing alongside the road, and a sizable distance from strip malls and highways – it got pretty quiet there.

I tried to get used to all of the beauty, but it was hard, particularly when I only had a bike and could not seem to pass my learner's permit test. When I got my first job at a grocery store, I learned the best way to bike the several miles to and from town. However, I still couldn't appreciate being outside. I was obsessed with the lameness of the activity, being seen on a bike outside instead of driving my own car. In the summer, the ride was often impossibly hot, and I would be sweating and huffing by the time I got to work. In the spring and fall, the rides home in the evening would be bitter cold and feel longer than ever.

During the summer before I left for college, I did start to feel a glimmer of *something* on my bike rides, not enjoyment for The Outdoors, exactly, but some sense of belonging or connection. I believed that I knew the route better than anyone and that made it feel like mine.

I applied to colleges just as *An Inconvenient Truth* was garnering buzz, and environmentalism became cool. I enrolled at an environmental college in central Vermont. I, of course, brought my little tabletop TV for the dorm, but the sound bothered my roommate when I left it on overnight. The first night I spent in the dorm room, television off and powerless, I cried and wished I were back in my bedroom at home.

The freshman course load included a required class called "Images of Nature" where the first assigned text was *A Sand County Almanac* by Aldo Leopold. I remember reading maybe half of the book and dismissing it. I liked Annie Dillard better anyway, with her sentences strung together like beads, each a beautiful, separate thing.

Everyday, we were led into conversations about the academic environment, the ways in which human beings were destroying the planet, and the will of nature over cities and towns. Not only in Images of Nature, but in my film history class and health classes, too. Essentially, these were blessed conversations that made a bunch of 18-year-olds feel like experts on the world. Still, I saw the outside as a place to smoke cigarettes with my friends, the Poultney River, located directly behind the campus, as a place to be seen in my bathing suit.

More than being lazy, which I was, my lack of appreciation seemed to stem from not being able to fathom why anyone would want to be outside by herself. It felt lonely out there in the world, without the company of boxed voices. I couldn't imagine driving to a trailhead, hiking to the summit, and being alone on top of a mountain. What would you do up there? Take a photograph? Journal? I seemed to equate comfort with company, and being outside seemed to only take me farther away from it.

A switch flipped for me in an environmental writing class in college. We drove as a class to a nearby nature preserve, and walked for several minutes out to a frozen field. We were instructed to find a place to sit, far enough away from anyone else so that you couldn't see or hear another soul. The class was asked to write about our impressions of the trees, the field, and the sky. We were not supposed to wander back to the meeting place for over an hour. The sun was starting to drop when we arrived, and any warmth left from the day was dissipating fast. I had worn an old down jacket and my leather sandals with socks. I had forgotten my hat and mittens. I settled down at the base of a skinny tree and huddled my legs. I rested my journal, which had "Nature Journal" emblazoned on the cover, on my lap.

I was immediately so cold that I couldn't hold my pen for any length of time and the writing in the journal looks like it was written in calligraphy. I kept looking around, looking to spot anyone who couldn't hack it and was walking back to sit in the van, as I longed to do, but there was no one in sight.

My self-conscious sentences ("I am trying to like the cold – to love it – but I don't yet." "There has to be deer because their shit is on the ground lying in patches of snow…") were meant to distract myself from my own mounting discomfort. I imagined telling this story when I got back to campus. I imagined how I might describe the field, crunchy with dirty snow and ice, or the sunset, which had broken the tin sky with a band of yellow at the horizon. There were a scattering of rotting apples around the base of the tree, so the air close to the ground smelled sickly sweet. My cheeks were cold and red, in a way I imagined was cute. I didn't consider that my nose would also be red and that the biting cold would make my raw dry skin ever dryer. I was feeling something similar to contentment in the discomfort, talking myself through the moment, providing my own company.

When the time was up, I shook out my legs and walked back to the van to sit and wait for the rest of my classmates. The inside of the van was too warm and shallow compared to the vast field and the sinking day. As everyone climbed inside, we all made "brrrrr" noises or raised our eyebrows, but then sat still in a charged silence.

After college, I kicked around and moved back home for a few months. There was only one television in the house, and the channels had been narrowed down to basic cable. Lonely again, I gobbled up books instead, taking them down to the New Haven River and lolling away whole afternoons on the rocks reading. I would often force myself out of the house during fall afternoons and evenings, when the air was cold and almost dark, to consider my life. The weird part was, it would sometimes work. Or better yet, the sound of my own steps, shuffling along and cracking over frozen mud puddles on the dirt road, would propel me out of my own head and I would just walk. Being lonesome made me less afraid of everything, and being lonely outside, with the company of, well, everything else, seemed preferable.

The appreciation for actually being outside came slowly, even slower than weaning myself off of television. As an adult, with both more and fewer choices for how to spend my time, I find that the more significant moments of my life rarely occur while I am stretched out on my couch. I believe that the greatest step towards appreciation and understanding of being outside has been giving up the idea of what I am supposed to love. I love walking outside, and riding my bike down a hill with no hands on the handlebars. I love swimming in rivers, and especially adore falling asleep next to them. I love the moment you get to sit at the top after an arduous hike, but dislike the moment you have to stand up and work your way down. Maybe I was programmed to love these things, but had no way of knowing until I did them over and over and felt better when I did. Maybe the hard work of people whose own finely developed love of being outdoors rubbed off on me, but I had to get past my own selfishness to notice.

I don't have a television now and allow myself only small doses. When I miss it, which I do sometimes when the night is too quiet, I try to remind myself that quiet is all right and that the world is bigger than a box.

Lené Gary

Lené Gary is a writer and poet living in the Green Mountains of Vermont. She holds an MFA in Creative Writing from Vermont College of Fine Arts and has won national literary awards for her poetry and prose. Her work has appeared in Birchsong: Poetry Centered in Vermont, Up the Staircase, Poemeleon, Limestone, Watershed, M Review, Pecan Grove Review, Connotation Press, SAGE, Vermont Nature, KNOCK, and others. When she's not writing, she can be found paddling her well-worn, Mad River canoe.

APOLOGY

The first time I heard them honking their way south was eleven years ago, when I was camping alone in the Green Mountains. I was a Texan then, just visiting Vermont, trying to decide if this small state would be my next home.

It was night. The moisture was so thick from the wet ground that my hair felt damp next to my skin. I listened from the warmth of my purple sleeping bag, my muscles alert, my mind a bit on edge from the proximity of these unfamiliar calls. It took three days before I knew they were geese. I overheard someone talking about their migration.

Geese. In the dark, chill-night of autumn, their calls woke me to this place and my out-of-place vulnerability.

Having grown up in Houston, where lights bled the stars away, where the sky-haze was simply a reflection of the pavement on which I walked, I never considered that the sky could also be a path for birds. A flyway. Until that fall.

The following year, I sold my house in Texas, having already lived in Vermont for several months. I was trying to wrap up those loose ends before my second "geese migration" came to a close.

I boarded the plane in San Antonio, whispering goodbye to the palm trees and mariachis. The fresh oysters, tortillas, and lightning storms. I knew I would miss the scrubby oaks and limestone hills. My pecan trees. I knew I'd miss the sun. And those crazy cowboys with their boots and hats in business suits. Bluebonnets and rodeos. So many things that made this place *this* place and no other—this Gulf Coast.

The engines roared, and as the gravitational pull sucked my body into the cloth-covered seat still warm from the passenger before, when I could no longer distinguish the sprawl of ranchettes from the window, I pulled closed the shade and opened my book. I had been waiting to read it. This was a gift to myself, a way of toasting what I believed was next.

The Snow Geese: A Story of Home.

I read the first chapter, learning that the house I had just sold in South Texas, a decision partially influenced by hearing the call of geese up north, was located within 120 miles of the place they overwinter.

That irony was not lost on me. *The home I had just sold was closer to geese than where I would live in Vermont, a place they were simply flying over.*

I could only laugh at myself and wonder why sometimes it takes moving 2,000 miles to find what is living in one's own backyard.

About 18 months later and on one of the first 50-degree days of 2005, my dear friend, Joel, and I headed out to Button Bay to celebrate the arrival of warmer temperatures.

I packed our lunches, my camera, our folding chairs— everything we needed. Birds were not on my brain like sunshine. It did not even occur to me to pack my binoculars; the lake was still frozen from what we'd heard.

Trekking the muddy, ice-patched path towards the lake, we heard the honking of geese in the distance, and it dawned on me: *they're back.*

I scanned the frozen bay, searching. Nothing but a dilapidated duck blind.

We kept walking.

Muddy ice held rotting leaves beneath red pines and empty oak trees. Oils of evergreens filled the air.

When we reached the tip of the small peninsula—an area of gray rock more like a whale's back--we could see a slippery place of water between ice flows.

Geese! Females popped in and out of the small obsidian waves. Males flapped and danced from the crouching island nearby, elongating their rubbery necks. Some of the females stood on the ice, facing south.

This was the first time I had seen geese returning instead of leaving. It took a few minutes for the experience to sink in—for me to realize that these were the same birds I was waving goodbye to in the

66

fall. That they were returning. That they were finding their way back to begin again.

I remember the sense of gratitude I had that day—for having found a place that woke me to birds. To the seasons. To my relationship with the natural world. And to a sense of wholeness in the midst of change.

That feels like a long time ago. This October marks eleven years since that first camping trip.

Joel is no longer with me (us); he's been gone six years. Since then, I've moved farther and farther from The Big Lake (what we call Lake Champlain), so there are fewer reminders of the seasonal rituals I shared with him. He was very much aware of the sky, the flyway—he lived in the valley along the lake.

I have thought about the geese this year, surprised that I haven't heard any calling. I've gone back to a few of the places Joel and I shared, happy to be in those places but not feeling particularly connected. It wasn't until I was asked to submit an essay about my relationship with the natural world that I deeply considered these things.

I opened my journals with the hope that I might find a starting point—a place to begin this essay. Reading through them, though, I was startled in the same way that I was by the calls of geese in 2002, when I didn't know what they were, but I wanted to know. When I didn't feel like I belonged, yet I wanted to belong.

When I opened my journals, I wanted to belong in *that* life, the one in which I had a real sense of what it meant to be living here, when I so sincerely felt a deep connection with the nonhuman world in which we co-exist, when I had someone special with whom to share those connections. I wanted to be back in that life.

Eleven years ago, geese woke me to the place I was living, my desire to know it more deeply, and my need for a sense of belonging within this world. This morning, my hand written reflections woke me much the same.

For years, I've believed in the power of stories, the way they can help us recover ourselves, but I didn't anticipate that when I opened my own story, it would be *my* way back. That it would help me recover myself, my sense of place in the deepest sense, and to find my friend.

I know if Joel were here, he'd be loading his old canoe, the one I have stored beside the house. He'd be telling me to grab my field guides, my binoculars, my notebook and pen. He would suggest gently yet firmly that I return to this relationship with open eyes and kindness, and apologize for leaving.

I know he's right.

I can't help but smile from the warmth of gratitude I hold under this gray day's hazy sun, loading his canoe onto my car, brushing the fallen leaves from the top of it, packing for the long road trip I'll make tomorrow. It's only October 4th. The geese are still moving.

Elvera Shappirio

Elvera Shappirio was born and has lived in Michigan for all but four years of her life. She has also lived in England and Belgium. She has a degree from the University of Michigan and has continued to study ever since. She spends as much time as possible outdoors, hiking, kayaking, identifying plants, bird-watching, and traveling in and out of Michigan. For the past 30 years she has been a potter and part owner of a cooperative Gallery.

GROWING UP OUTDOORS IN MICHIGAN

I have always had a passion for the out-of-doors. I love all the birds, animals, insects and plants. Being outdoors is comforting and walking in the woods is especially fascinating as I study everything around me. Learning to identify just about everything is my hobby.

I grew up on a farm in Michigan during the Depression and World War II.

I know that I spent a great deal of time outdoors as a young child, probably from the time I could walk. There are stories about me carrying a can of chicken feed around the yard so I could feed the chickens who were also free to roam around the yard. The rooster attacked me so he became chicken stew. He was a tough old bird with long dangerous spurs.

At this time, when I was about two years old, I apparently used to wander down the lane toward the pasture field, which was probably a quarter of a mile from the barn, to explore. My father might be working in the field next to it with the horses doing plowing or raking or whatever had to be done in the fields. He would keep an eye on me as I wandered back up the lane. If the cows happened to come up the lane to be milked and saw me there they would come up behind me and sniff me and maybe knock me down, not really injuring me, but they couldn't figure out what I was. After this happened my parents decided it was time to allow the cows to become acquainted with me. I went into the barn with my father while the cows were in their stalls ready to be milked and he introduced me to the cows by letting me be in front of the cows while they were eating and then in back of the cows with my father while he was milking them by hand. After observing for a while I apparently walked into a stall figuring I would be able to milk a cow too. The cow had other ideas and kicked me out of the stall. I remember landing against the wall. I was not injured but my father had to rearrange his plans a little so that wouldn't happen again.

Eventually, I had two sisters two and four years younger than I was. After a few years when they were old enough we would all wander off together to explore. Sometimes we would go back in the woodlot or we would walk along the hedgerows at the edges of the fields. We explored the pasture field among the cows who would ignore us as if we were part of the scenery. I can remember lifting small stones to see what the ants under them were doing. There were Bobolinks singing in the hayfields and blue birds nesting in holes in the fence posts.

Sometimes there were Turkey Vultures sitting on the fence posts looking mournfully at us. They were fairly ugly but they seemed friendly or tolerant of us. When we approached them they would fly away and settle down a bit further away.

My parents were able to identify all of the common birds and animals so we learned from them. They also knew the common insects and native plants. There were many European weeds. We always asked which ones we could eat and nibbled on all of those. Dandelion greens are very bitter. Milkweed is beyond bitter even after it has been boiled in two changes of water and then poached in milk. Cheese grass and plantain seeds have very little flavor. Cooked Purslane is not bad and Lamb's Quarters is good. Amaranth is even better. There were berries to be picked too. Apples, pears and cherries from an old unsprayed orchard made good eating. The applesauce made from several old apple varieties was wonderful. Perhaps the wormy apples made it better.

There was a large vegetable garden from which we ate fresh vegetables in season and canned and preserved for winter consumption. Picking and cutting up green beans for canning was not a favorite task for me. I also didn't like to pick up potatoes. They were stored in a large pile in the cellar to be eaten all winter.

Some days my father would say, as we finished dinner, "Well, I don't hear the cows coming up the lane. Do you want to go down to the pasture and bring them up?" We did. It was wonderful running down the lane in the late afternoon, hearing the birds and seeing some small animals. The cows would seem to be saying, "Oh yes, it is that time isn't it?" and we would follow them as they all went into the barn to be milked. Most of the time the cows came to the barn at milking time because they were ready to be milked

When we were old enough we would go through the woods to the neighbors' property to visit the old White Pine tree, which was a relic from the pre-lumbering days.

Eventually we went through the neighbors' property to property we owned down the road a bit, where we explored the edges of an extensive bog. On one exploration early in the spring there were Fairy shrimp in the small pools of water and frogs singing. We noticed that the frogs stopped singing when we just walked by, then they began again after we were far enough away. Later there were six or seven different kinds of snails in the water. Sometimes they laid small gelatinous masses of eggs.

When we tired of exploring we would return home the way we had gone there through the woods and fields rather than taking the road. On one occasion when we were getting much older I got myself disoriented and we found ourselves on a road 2 1/2 miles from our home. I still remember how tired I was when we got home. My sisters were young enough to just depend on me to get them home.

Our brother, who was 10 years younger than I, eventually grew old enough to go with us on our excursions. To this day he complains that he was always the last in line and branches were allowed to snap back in his face because no one was paying attention to him. He was still small so the branches were on his level.

My sisters and I attended a one-room country school which was three quarters of a mile from our farm. We walked to and from school even in the winter. When my father was asked why he didn't drive us home, he replied that we would certainly want to play outdoors until dinner time so it wasn't necessary. We agreed with that since it was true. We certainly did enjoy playing outside when we could, even in very cold snowy weather.

There were never more than twenty-one students in the school from six families.

During the school day there was a recess in the morning and a lunch hour plus a recess in the afternoon. While we were outdoors we were mostly unsupervised so we played games that didn't lead to too much conflict such as "Kick the Can", "Prisoners goal", "Softball" (if some one brought a ball and bat), or we explored the schoolyard and nearby property. Sometimes the teacher had to intervene in disputes.

Walking to and from school was interesting.

We occasionally saw neighbors who lived in the four farms on our way and we paid attention to whatever tasks they might be engaged in. One family had a small flock of Guinea hens. The hens marched about proclaiming "poe tek, poe tek" endlessly. We loved them. We could not hear them from our house.

Another neighbor raised turkeys. These birds were very nervous, noisy and afraid of everything. We were admonished to avoid annoying them in any way as we walked by that farm. Those neighbors were also reputed to dislike children. We were careful.

When I was a child, gardening was a necessary activity for the family but I found it to be tedious. As an adult I developed a passion for it. I raise vegetables in "Earthboxes." The yard is full of all sorts of shrubs and flowers including some prairie plants.

As I have written about my childhood I have realized that I have continued to do all of the kinds of things I did as a child, and my husband shared all of these interests. We live in town but we are near an old woodlot. We both became "birdwatchers" and enjoyed exploring lake edges, woods and prairies.

Isaac Yelchin

I grew up in the streams and ponds. Frogs, lizards, snakes, skinks, and the like are my favorite. Any opportunity to get my hands on a little guy I go for. This passion has inspired me to express my love of nature in every walk of life. My art to my jobs I try my best to be involved in the outdoors.

NATURE'S LAWS

Thanks to my man Frank, (Frank Baele, my sophomore and junior year science teacher) I was able to ID and try to snook a garter snake, (snook is my word for catching snakes) a non-venomous black snake with occasional white stripes on its flank. The garter snake likes to hang about water in hopes of catching some little frogs or fish to fill its 3-foot belly. I ventured down into the riverbed to nab the little guy, managed to place myself in perfect catching position (squatted-hunched-bent-heeled over, hands-free hovering, ready to strike, pounce capture my prey, my joy, my reward for my tracking), and I told myself, "Go," here's your chance the snake is motionless, in easy reach. GO! But GO, is not what I did. What I did was lame. I slowly reached out for it. Of course, the snake hightailed it out of the creek when it saw my hand approaching. It had an easy escape for my hand was moving so slow I swear it was going backwards. Now that seems like a story of me blabbing about how I chickened out on catching a snake. And well yeah, it is. But the important thing is how I was brought to that point. Because in the past, when I was six or seven or eight or nine, maybe ten, I was able to pick up snakes just like I do a frog or a lizard, all the same ritual and preparation and then the strike

74

the combination of speed and accuracy of my hand and the gentle capture of the animal that makes me unique, I seemed to completely forget when snooking this garter snake. I blame that rattlesnake that damn near killed my brother.

Three years ago a rattlesnake bit my little brother Ezra who was two at the time. It happened at our home, in Topanga Canyon, a low mountain woodland area near the heart of Los Angeles, while he was with his babysitter. While in class I received a phone call from my dad informing me of Ezra's injury. We live on a road that is bumpy, like in a park, and an ambulance might have had difficulty navigating the turns, so my dad took my brother to an urgent care center, but they did not have the proper medical equipment to treat him. They sent for an ambulance to take Ezra to the hospital. Because of the delay, the poison traveled further up his leg, raising the risk of it reaching his heart. He stayed in the ICU for a week and received the same dosage of anti-venom given to an adult, 40 vials. His foot became so swollen that he had surgery to avoid nerve damage. He survived, but is still suffering from the bite; Ezra now has Post Traumatic Stress Disorder, and this has taken a toll on our family. His resulting behavioral problems make it difficult at times for our family to function smoothly.

Slinking, slithering, tongue-flicking, devilish, rattlesnakes have complex nervous systems they can hear through their jaws. They lay eggs that are watertight, one more daily fact. In most cultures the snake is viewed as an evil being, symbolizing death. It is the Year of the Snake in China, but the creature is not well liked by the Chinese. According to the *Wall Street Journal* Chinese businesses' efforts to sell snake toys and memorabilia have been unsuccessful, so they've turned to marketing Valentine's Day chocolates instead. Throughout history snakes have been viewed as the Devil's animal, or Satan himself. In the Book of Genesis the serpent ruins Adam and Eve's innocent life in Eden.

I'm sad to say that a snake caused my fall from the Eden of Topanga. Even now as I write this, I feel slightly sick from retelling the events. While my brother was in physical therapy learning to walk again, I couldn't fathom returning to my ways of catching lizards and garter snakes. Of course I didn't always feel this. At first it seemed that I lived in harmony with nature and I had no fear of it. Observing a Western Fence Lizard do pushups in the sun or finding a croaking frog perched on a stick was my favorite pastime. I hiked seasonal creeks in search of salamanders. When coming home from school on a late rainy night I would stop so I could watch a frog jumping across our road to the creek below. My engagement with nature wasn't always so benign. Once while trying to catch a lizard that ran beneath one of my dad's unpainted canvases, I was confronted with a hissing rattlesnake. This pit viper is deadly so I dropped the canvas and jumped back, forgetting the lizard.

Nonetheless my family and I have lived alongside nature with relative ease. Even though honeybees once built a hive in the ceiling of our house and honey dripped down the walls, I transported by hand piles of living and dead bees from the floor to the outdoors. In 5th grade when my friend and I were digging out a mud fort at the base of a culvert at the rear of my house, a live grey scorpion appeared in one of our scoopers. We just set it back where we'd uncovered it and continued to dig. Tarantulas, horny toads, garter snakes – I've caught them with bare hands and marveled at their gentleness.

But slowly, in time, I've felt the same calling again. However my connection to nature has matured, perhaps now out of respect for nature's laws. My favorite class, Field Biology, has taught me the way of a naturalist, which is based in knowing the limits of engagement with nature. I now understand how connected every act of engagement is. Yet I worry that we as a society have not learned to respect nature's laws. Take for example the effects of modern industry's release of carbon dioxide gas into the air. The result is that our planet is heating up. The planet must be able to cool itself off if it is to maintain homeostasis, one of nature's laws. But instead polar ice caps are melting. This melting diminishes the surface area of white on the planet, which would reflect light from the sun. More sun exposure heats up the earth at an ever-increasing rate. Drastic weather such as Hurricanes Sandy and Katrina is just one result of our earth overheating. As a human race we need to learn to respect nature's laws or else it is sure to bite us back.

Carla Brown

Carla Brown is a Maker in all areas of her life. She builds digital products at the National Wildlife Federation. She designs activities for families to enjoy nature. She creates beautiful and useful things from trash, which she documents at her blog, www.trashmagination.com. She loves making the most resonant sounds and rhythms with other Taiko drum musicians. She cultivates a rich family life with her husband Bob, daughter Nora and son Russell. She is still grateful after all these years for the opportunity to attend Lester B. Pearson College on full scholarship as the representative from Nova Scotia. She sends many hugs across the planet to her fellow hikers - Sherie, Theron and Roberto.

CHOOSING WHEN TO LET GO

One reason we turn to nature is to feel fully alive.

When I was a teenager, I attended a school that focused on living in the moment. Lester B. Pearson College in British Columbia encouraged us to kayak, hike, climb – where we pushed ourselves and worked as a team. During one of these hikes, I had what might be called a "rite of passage" moment.

Friends and I decided to hike the West Coast Trail. It was an exhausting trip – climbing 30-foot ladders up steep hillsides, walking on rocky beaches, sleeping in a lean-to or cave. Despite our preparations, we were cold and wet for much of the week. Our skin on our backs chafed from being wet while carrying heavy packs.

There were sweet moments as well, such as when Roberto sang opera with his tremendous voice on the shore as the sun was setting. Or when we found a cave and were able to dry out every piece of clothing, especially socks. Or when a fellow hiker gave us a Sterno can when we were struggling to start a fire. And of course, the never-ending beauty of the ancient rainforest right beside the Pacific Ocean.

After almost a week, we reached the end of the 75 kilometer-long trail. The trailhead is at one side of a very large river called the Gordon River, and the only way to leave the trail is to get a boat across. A few times a day, there is a man with a boat who looks across the river. If someone wants transport, they hoist a flag and he will come.

Unfortunately, when we reached the trailhead, it was stormy at sea. The waves were large. When the boat driver got close to shore, he shouted that he could not bring the boat to shore because the waves would make it impossible to get the boat back out. He asked if we wanted to sleep there and he would come back tomorrow, or whether we wanted to try a riskier way of getting in the boat. It involved climbing out on a rocky overhang where he could drive underneath, and we would then fall into his boat from above.

We desperately wanted to get off the trail, so we opted for the cliff. He said the waves come in patterns, and that we should let the first few wash over us so we know when to let go. He said to fall after three waves hit us so he knew when to bring the boat closest in. I think it was Roberto who went first, and I saw the waves wash up over his entire body. I thought it would pull him off the cliff but he held on, and then successfully dropped the 10-15 feet into the boat.

With my giant packsack on, I climbed down slowly from the top of the cliff. When the first cold wave hit, it whooshed up over my body and into my eyes and ears. The salt stung every sore spot on my body. Two more waves, and then I just let go. I fell with a thud in the boat. It was the most intense nature experience I ever had, pushing me beyond what I thought was possible physically.

These days, when I explore nature with my family, almost every moment is photographed because we have so many devices. Back then, I did not own a camera and so I have no photos from this experience. It is interesting how this total lack of documentation makes it seem almost like it did not happen. The only item I have that proves it was real was the tattered library book about how to hike the trail that we brought with us.

Mary Fancher

Mary Fancher spent early years in New Jersey where she had a favorite tree to climb. During teen years she lived in Florida where she tried over and over to climb a coconut palm barefoot and failed. In New Mexico she searched in vain for trees. Now, in Michigan, she watches the trees outside the window and enjoys their seasonal changes.

OUT THE DOOR

Just as kids today can't imagine growing up without television and video games, I can't imagine how they can sit looking at an animated screen when there is so much to do outside. I had the good fortune to grow up in a very small town during a time when kids went outdoors in the morning, ran home for a hurried lunch, and didn't return until "the whistle blew" for dinner. All mothers had a whistle and all kids knew which special code to answer.

Every time I went out the door, even when walking to school, I became an explorer. The whole outdoors became my place to learn, to observe, to experiment, to question. What does skunk cabbage smell like up close? What happens when rabbits see the bean shoots in the garden? What happens if I pick wildflowers and bring them inside? How far can that ant carry the large crumb before dropping it? Which clouds promise a storm? What do I do when I finally haul myself up on a branch and am afraid to jump down? In learning these things I was also learning about myself and having to make my own decisions. And yes, I did jump off the branch and despite a few scrapes it was not so bad after all. In fact I did it again and again.

"Mom, I'm bored," I said as I followed her around the house.

"Clean up your room," was one of her standard answers.

"I did that already and I'm still bored."

"Go out and play." No offers to come out with me and tell me what to do, what to play, how to play. But I didn't want her company outdoors and preferred being on my own. What did we do outside? All sorts of things. We adapted what we did to fit the seasons.

SUMMER

Usually we began our day by knocking on another kid's door and asking if he or she could play. We did not have play dates arranged by parents. If we could get enough kids –usually five were enough for a game, boys or girls –we would play baseball. Pitcher, batter, catcher and a couple of outfielders. We played in the street and someone always could find a piece of cardboard to put over the sewer opening to keep the ball from disappearing. I was the only lefty in town and had my own left-handed mitt. No one else could ever borrow it.

Roller-skating was popular, also in the street. We could not wear tennis shoes for that since the skates had to be clamped and locked onto hard shoes. One summer I spent so much time on skates that it felt weird to take them off. I was not allowed to skate in the house and until we added a small bathroom by the side door I would have to crawl across the living room and up the stairs. I could have taken off the skates but it was more fun the other way. On rare occasions someone's parent would agree to let us hang on to their slow moving car for a few blocks of being towed on skates –but I probably should not mention that. Not a good idea anymore.

We had a Victory Garden, as so many families did during the years of WWII. I remember the fun of sticking a shovel into the dirt under the potato plants and turning over a spade full of tiny potatoes. I also remember demanding money to pull the ugly green tomato worms off tomato plants. Probably a penny per or maybe even a nickel, but I would not do it for free.

Our back yard provided me with a large weeping willow tree where I could crawl under the branches and feel hidden from the world. While there I could read or lie down and daydream, or, if my older brother were feeling generous I could play with his toy soldiers and trucks. (I know, I should have had my own set.)

Along one fence we grew Concord grapes. In the summer I would sit in the grass, suck the inside out of the ripe grapes and see how far I could spit the sour skin.

Behind the yard and garden we had glorious woods. In the woods there were trees to climb, a small brook perfect for building dams, wild berries, and poison ivy, the last not a pleasant memory but it taught me how to identify it in the future.

Sometimes in the summer we would drive from New Jersey to Michigan and visit my grandmother in Muskegon, near Lake Michigan. She had a cottage set at one end of a semi circle of a dozen other places, on a small lake that fed into the Big Lake, as we called it. I never really learned to swim anything but sidestroke there but it was enough to be allowed to the end of the dock in the deep water. One had to be able to swim from shore out and around the front of the dock to qualify. We loved to jump off the dock and wash our hair in the cold lake at night.

Our town, though small, had clay tennis courts. We all played tennis at varying levels and all had a good time. For our informal lessons I, with my left hand, always had to stand at the end of the line that stretched across the court. I never minded and always felt special.

Bike riding took up a large part of our time outdoors. We rode anywhere and everywhere around town. Riding no handed was a special thrill, especially when plunging down steep Tank Hill. No helmets – how did we survive?

AUTUMN

In the fall things changed and school took over most of our free time. Still we managed to be outside (after coming home and changing clothes) until the whistle for dinner. We still played ball, tennis, rode bikes and skated, but soon we had leaves. And we raked them into large piles and threw ourselves into them, buried each other in them, and argued over who could be first to jump into a newly raked mountain of leaves. We would throw a small ball into the pile and try to be the one who found it.

We played tag, hide-and-seek, statues, and many variations of those games. Sometimes we made our own rules, and argued about them. Again, no parents came out to settle our disagreements, we made it work. Almost every back yard had a swing set with a slide and I could spend a long time swinging back and forth. I liked to twist the swing until the chains were tight and then spin around as it unwound. As I got older I liked to swing high and jump off at the top of the swing.

WINTER

And now, winter, and outdoor activities did not come to a halt in the cold weather. The snow was our toy and we played in and with it endlessly. We built forts and had snowball battles, we built snowmen of all sizes. The snowman's body was made of three large balls of graded sizes and sometimes we made the base so large that it was hard to get the next ball or tummy part on top of it. Often that part would disintegrate as we tried to pick it up and we would start all over again. Pebbles from the driveway for eyes and mouth and the usual carrot nose under an old hat and scarf.

Just as we had jumped into piles of leaves we now threw ourselves into mountains of snow. We made snow angels, trying hard to get up without leaving any other marks around them. We went sledding in the streets, ice skating on the pond in the golf course and skiing down the hill in front of the Wheeler's house. A few years ago I made a brief visit to my small hometown and was amazed at how tiny our skiing hill looked. We felt we were zooming down a mountain and were thrilled.

One bitterly cold year my older brother and I built an igloo at the end of the driveway. We made blocks of snow, poured cups of water over them to freeze and soon had enough to make a small igloo with room for one at a time. It was scary (for me) to crawl through the short tunnel entrance, turn and sit inside. I never stayed long.

Our house had a small greenhouse attached to the dining room. It received the full afternoon sun and was warm enough for play on cold days. There were long boxes constructed to hold the soil so my father could start the plants for the spring garden. He let us use the parts he didn't need for our games. We weren't really outside but we had soil and cars and it smelled like the outdoors and the dirt got under our fingernails. I loved to construct roads with curves and hills and used small mirrors for lakes.

SPRING

Spring arrived and there was plenty of work to do, helping with the new garden, deciding which vegetables to grow. I always wanted beans and tomatoes in my small section and eggplant was not allowed. I might have to eat the requisite three bites when it was served for dinner (swallowing each bite whole with a big gulp of milk) but I was not going to grow it in my garden.

Spring was also the time to get the bikes out of the garage and check the brakes, put air in the tires, and if we had grown, raise the seat and handlebars. It was time to see if we had forgotten how to ride during the long winter. That never happened.

DIFFERENT NATURAL ENVIRONMENTS

During high school years I lived in Florida where I still spent most of my free time outdoors. I spent many afternoon hours trying to teach myself how to play golf. With a driver, cotton golf balls, and an open book by Ben Hogan or Sam Snead lying on the grass, I would practice my swing over and over. Finally my grandmother offered me real lessons and soon we were going out each weekend for our nine holes of golf. We were about equal in ability, so both of us enjoyed it.

The rest of my free time I spent at the beach. It was the place to be for a teenager. We could play with the waves (unless there had been a jellyfish alert) and come out to sit on the beach towel, leaving the salt water on our hair. We believed it helped turn our hair blond.

In Florida I learned about hurricanes and their circular winds. I tried going out in the yard during one to find out if the strong winds could hold me up if I leaned back. During the eye of one hurricane that hit us directly I went for a brief bike ride, with the warning to hurry back when the winds started up again. I will always associate the smell of rotting foliage with that time, when no leaves moved and the birds had disappeared.

During college years my time outdoors was spent walking the mile to my classes and back, usually four times a day, three days a week. When I started dating the fellow who would become my future husband, one of our early outings was unusual. He liked to fish, I had never been fishing but had always wanted to go, ever since my father had taken my brother on a trip to Nova Scotia and I was ruled too young to accompany them. My date wanted to go fishing on a Sunday morning, I was agreeable, but first we had to have bait. So our Saturday night out was a trip to the University of Michigan baseball field equipped with a flashlight and old coffee can with dirt in it. I was instructed in the method for catching night crawlers, which are long fat worms. At night they liked to poke their heads or top part out of the ground. Trying not to scare them, I was to approach, grab on to the part showing and pull it out of the ground. Well, I was worried that if I held on too tightly the poor worm would squish in my fingers. So most of my attempts failed as the worm easily pulled out of my grasp and retreated underground. I did manage to get a few as I grew more daring, but I can't say it was very enjoyable.

Fishing became a main activity when our children were young and we often spent a Saturday at a nearby lake with our rowboat and a picnic lunch. But those are their stories to tell.

I realize that a lot of this would sound boring to today's children and I am sure we were bored some of the time too. It is hard to convey the way I felt during my time as a kid outdoors. I was free, I had to make my own decisions about what to do and how to do it. I did not have many wildlife encounters while outside, never went hunting, had an aversion to too many bugs, although it was fun to lie in the grass and watch them on their travels. The whole outdoors was my learning lab –I could plant some seeds and check on them every day waiting for the first little green shoots to appear. I learned which berries were safe to eat and which plants to avoid. I learned about building a small dam in a creek and what the water would do to avoid being trapped by it.

Nowadays, some 65 to 70 years later, my explorations are much more limited. No more jumping into the leaf pile, roller skating, or playing in the Atlantic Ocean. I have been lucky enough to have seen the Grand Canyon, walked on the shores of the Pacific, strolled among the giant Sequoias of California, and gazed in awe at the power of Niagara Falls, and in wonder at the Alps. I have climbed trees in the woods behind our house in New Jersey, built sand castles on the beach in Florida, experienced the power of a dust storm in New Mexico and a hurricane in Florida. In South Africa I had the unforgettable experience of seeing the wild animals as they should be seen, in their own surroundings and not the artificial ones of a zoo. The ranger driving the camp vehicle kept the engine running and was poised to flee as we watched an elephant pull up a small tree and strip its branches of bark and leaves. I watched and listened to the crunch as a leopard in a tree feasted on a warthog. A rhinoceros family showed us its family values as Mama frolicked with her cute new baby as older brother tried to join them. Each time he approached, Mama would stomp toward him, driving him back. As they traveled through the meadow brother followed, many yards behind, head hanging.

Each place I've lived or visited has had its own special beauty and I want these experiences and resources available to future generations. Perhaps without the dust storms.

BACKYARD WILDLIFE

In our backyard in Michigan we observe wildlife, perhaps a groundhog, rabbits, squirrels, birds and chipmunks, an occasional raccoon and we hope not a skunk.

One spring I bought a new bird feeder. When we lost our ash tree we also lost a feeder which had hung from a lower branch, not the best location for the birds because of squirrel competition, but the best for our viewing. We had missed the birds this past winter and decided to invite them back to the yard.

Taking the place of the tree we now have a black pole with hooks for hanging two of the long cylinder feeders, one filled with thistle and the other with either sunflower seeds or a mixture of several kinds. We hope the baffle, another cylinder, defeats the squirrels. The feeder is near some bushes and fairly near our back windows, where we sit to eat our meals.

No birds came the first day, but by the second morning every perch was taken and the birds, mostly finches and cardinals, were enjoying a meal. Our resident chipmunk, Alvin, came to check out his chances of joining the dinner hour. He ran easily up the pole, continued climbing inside the baffle, bumping his head at the top. Down he came, turned around and tried again. He did this several times, finally stopping near the bottom of the baffle, stretching his paws toward the outside of it, but unable to grab hold. He sat in the yard, thinking deeply about his problem while eyeing the feeders and the happy birds, eating away. Then he scrambled up and out to the edges of the nearby bush but the branch ends would not hold him. Back to the ground for more studying of the situation. He climbed up the clothes pole, a circular one, ran out to the end of one spoke, then another. But it was too far to jump. We had to leave the window then, and at last sight he was sitting on the tree stump, with his back to the feeders, frowning and looking peevish.

So far the squirrels are busy burying nuts and are not very hungry for birdseed. But we are worried. The cable TV line runs above the new feeders. Chipmunks don't usually walk on wires, but squirrels do, and they love to jump and cling to feeders. And my learning about the ways of the outdoors and its inhabitants continues, even as a spectator sport, one created to enjoy this smaller version of the natural world.

Barbara Debrodt

The author grew up in an alley-deprived suburb of Pittsburgh, Pennsylvania, so the games described are courtesy of her husband of 58 years, Robert E. Debrodt. He played them all in Detroit, Michigan. And enjoyed them all. They have lived in Ann Arbor, Michigan, ever since they married, at times working at the University of Michigan (Bob as Director of Development Legal Services, the author as a television producer), and as UM students, (the author got a law degree there at the age of 50). She put that education to work first as Assistant Legal Counsel to Michigan Governor William G. Milliken, and later as a county prosecutor.

ALLEY GAMES

Alas, I grew up in a semi-posh neighborhood where there were no alleys. I didn't know it, but I was deprived. My husband, however, was not so unfortunate. Where he grew up, many decades ago on the west side of Detroit, Michigan, there were alleys, some paved, some unpaved, roadways that cut a block in half and were fronted by garages and two-holed garbage cans.

And there were children, mostly boys but a few intrepid girls. And it was in the alleys where those children could play, without supervision by adults or coaches. Marbles, of course, and one-man catch, where the player would bounce a tennis ball off a garage door and then catch it, again and again.

But it was the team games that he remembers well. "Duck on a Rock" was one. It was a variation of "Tag" in which one person was "IT", and put an empty condensed milk can on a brick in the middle of

90

the alley and closed his eyes. Then he called out, "One, two, three, here I come!" The other players, also with cans, ran and hid. IT then went looking for the hiders and when he found one, both he and the hider raced to the brick, the hider at the same time throwing his/her can, trying to knock IT's can off the brick.

If the hider knocked IT's can off the brick, he/she was "Safe" and IT had to go looking for another hider. But if IT got to the brick first and shouted, "One, two, three" while striking the brick with the can three times before the hider could knock it off, IT won and the loser became IT for the next game.

"Tippie" was a game modeled on baseball. It was played with a six to seven inch piece of broomstick, called a "Tippie", and one of full length for a bat. To start the game, the short piece was leaned against the long side of a brick. An "outfield" was marked in the dirt, (or with chalk on a concrete surface) producing three oblongs, each farther away from the brick, with the farthest about two house lots deep.

A player with the full-size broomstick started by tipping the smaller piece on its high end, then hitting it again as though hitting a baseball, sending it sailing through the air. If the flying Tippie landed in the closest oblong, it was a Single, the next, a Double, the next a Triple, and beyond that a Home Run. If the Tippie landed outside the oblongs (or through a neighbor's window) it was an Out.

"Cable" was a variation of "Tippie" and involved playing with a hard baseball. Players wore baseball gloves, if they had them! The game required two vertically parallel wires strung high across the alley, probably a telephone wire and a power wire, one above the other, about three inches apart and joined by tying a vertical wire about every six to eight feet, to hold them together. Again, the alley surface was marked off as in "Tippie" with the closest oblong being a Single, etc. The player would throw the ball at the cable. If his opponent missed catching it, it was a hit. If the ball got stuck in between the two wires of the cable, it was a home run.

They played touch football, of course. (No tackling!) They also played marbles but called the game "Agates." They went roller-skating in the streets, if their parents or a policeman didn't come along and stop them.

They even went rat hunting. This was an evening activity and the hunters used a flashlight to shine into garbage cans where the rats' eyes would shine back and give them away. For a weapon, the hunters pounded a large nail into a piece of wood, usually a broomstick, which they used as a spear. This, I presume, was a boys-only pastime!

Meantime in the wealthier neighborhoods, we had to make do with playing house in an abandoned stone quarry, picking violets, and exploring the dense foliage in the ravine in the back of our house. How does that compete with rat hunting? No contest!

Eugenie Doyle

Eugenie Doyle is the author of two novels, a picture book, and numerous short stories, most set on farms. She and her family operate an organic vegetable, berry, and hay farm in Vermont.

INHERITING AN OUTDOOR LIFE

My parents, aged 92 and 93, recently sold the house of my childhood. No family member was at the closing, or rather, the theft, where the buyers paid very little to the old couple needing to be rid of the burden of a big, old house on eight acres, all needing care. Especially the old couple. None of my four siblings nor I wanted the place. We have our own places. I have a farm.

I took what I wanted: a few family pictures, including a portrait of my unsmiling 19-year-old great grandmother painted shortly before her death. I was named after her. She reminds me of legacy, of mortality and of artful love, for the frame carved by her grieving husband is exquisite.

I took the pictures and I took my childhood: a long, long period of playful freedom and creative loneliness lived almost entirely outside. The former small dairy farm included on its eight acres a barn with horse and cow stalls, three decrepit chicken coops, a shed full of play possibilities, and an outhouse. There was a vegetable garden, pear, apple, and peach trees, an asparagus patch, currant bushes, flowerbeds, a perennial rock garden, a clover field, and a compost heap. There were several springs, a frog pond, and a long section of brook. Playthings all to five children with busy, working parents.

There was a towering, eminently climbable pine tree from which I could spy on the wealthier neighbor's pool. At least, their daughter, one year my senior, claimed that her father was richer than mine. She had a horse so she was probably right.

I never got a horse although I filled the barn and field with imaginary ones. Imaginary chickens in the coops. The garden produced real vegetables; I became a good weeder, and lover of fresh food. We would begin dinner by naming the things on our plate that we had grown: *our own zucchini, our own raspberries.* Always proud, always delighted.

That delight propelled me to a life as a vegetable and berry grower. I married a man who also grew up outside.

Our home is haphazardly furnished. We have no flair for interior decorating. It seems, even after 34 years, to be temporary. My great grandmother's stern gaze seems disapproving of her new lodging. I can only imagine her tidy home and the workshop of the artist who made her exquisite frame.

My true home is outside in lush, eternally changing, productive fields.

Kathleen McKinley Harris

Kathleen McKinley Harris grew up in a family of nature lovers. Her parents became Audubon members in 1938. She is a Middlebury graduate and has a master's in English from Case Western Reserve University. She has taught kindergarten, high school English and history, and has acted in and directed plays. She co-owned and reported for and edited a semi-weekly newspaper. She is a gardener and skier. Her picture book, "The Wonderful Hay Tumble," was published by William Morrow, Jr. Her poetry has been published in "Vermont Life," "Snowy Egret," and "The Comstock Review," and "The Society of Children's Writers and Illustrators Bulletin."

EARLY MORNING WALKS

Our beloved, only grandparent, he lived on his Lake Ontario fruit farm as a widower with his eldest son, son's wife, and two of our cousins. He loved the land. His father's poor health had made it necessary for Grandpa to assume the management of his family's three farms while he was still at the academy —equivalent to present day high school and the first two years of college. His father, who had asthma, moved to North Carolina in an effort to improve his health and entrusted his business to his son. Grandpa was a fine student, but his love of the natural world was so keen he refused to go to Cornell University when his parents wanted him to attend. He said he couldn't bear to be cooped up indoors when spring came. I imagine, too, he had become accustomed as an 18-year-old to measuring up to a grown man's responsibilities.

My sister, Jane, and I knew it was Grandpa's lifelong habit to rise at 4 a.m. because he believed the best hours of the day were before noon. Every day at his lake home he took a walk on his land to Lake Ontario's shore. Always he made discoveries.

When he visited our home, he took his usual morning walk. Jane and I always planned to join him on his walk, but as young children, our heads stuck fast to our pillows. If we did stumble bleary-eyed out of bed early, we always were a few minutes late: Grandpa was out of sight. Later, at the breakfast table, his face a-glow from exercise and smelling of fresh air, he'd tell of his adventures and we'd be envious.

Then one morning when we were vacationing in Hyde Park, Vermont, Jane and I did get up on time to join Grandpa. He beamed at us, delighted to have our company at such an early hour. It was as if he couldn't imagine better companions. We each had orange juice and a bite to eat. We put on jackets and boots. It was chilly from night although it was the middle of summer.

So the three of us headed out. I felt as if we were putting something over the rest of the family who were still asleep. Grandpa tucked a couple of plastic bread bags into his pocket—"in case I find something I want to take home."

The sun was still hidden behind the hill in the east. Fog lay in thick banks over the mountain range in the west. The landscape at dawn was strange, completely different from later in the day. It was as if we were walking onto the edge of a white sea. The highest hills on the horizon across the valley were islands rising out of white water.

"We're walking through a cloud," I said as white, wet, feathery wisps of fog hit my face. I tried to brush away the whiteness; it blurred my vision. Heavy dew covered every blade of grass, and I was glad for boots.

"Now, girls, we need to be quiet and not scare away the animals. Maybe we'll see something." He led the way single file across the road into the cow pasture. He took us to the edge of a clearing, pointed out a sandy hump which he said was one entrance to a fox den. Later he pointed out matted down long grasses and whispered, "Deer bed." He raised his finger to his lips to hush our talking.

As soundlessly as we could, we followed him to the other side of a huge boulder. He stopped suddenly. We almost piled into him. We looked where he was gazing. Nestled near the rock was a reddish, spotted fawn. We went no closer. The memory of the delicate, quiet creature remains. Then Grandpa led us back the way we'd come.

He took us through a swampy place of sedges, reeds, and ferns. Black muck sucked at our boots. I was afraid I'd lose a boot. He picked some mint, gave us some to taste. He tucked some mint into one of his bags. He showed us how to recognize the mint family from its square stem.

Of course, we picked flowers for the breakfast table as we hiked home. He often brought back flowers for Mother. I felt starved and happy about what we'd experienced before the world was awake. The mountain islands of dawn were gone because the fog ocean had vanished. But the memory of what we'd experienced in Grandpa's company on that walk and many others remains and influences how I spend some of my best hours.

Jan Hudson Krueger

Jan Hudson Krueger is a retired elementary school teacher and a happily married mother of two grown children. She had the good fortune to be raised in a rural setting in Ontario, Canada. In addition, she spent every summer of her life at a remote family cottage in the north-central part of the province. Jan has lived with her family for the past 38 years in southwestern Ontario. She continues to write stories, poems and articles, often with a nod toward natural science. Armed with her cameras and binoculars, she is always up for a road trip, no matter the length, just to get "out there" and see what natural wonders she can discover.

PASSION

Passion. I think that's mostly what it takes to get our kids outside, unplugged from their indoor devices and plugged into Nature.

I was most fortunate to have been raised by parents who were amateur ornithologists, horticulturalists and naturalists. The back part of my home property was part of a huge woodlot, complete with a hurricane-tumbled ravine and a small, safe but dark creek snaking along the bottom. And this was only about a half a mile up from the shores of Lake Ontario. I spent the entirety of every summer at a remote family cottage up in the Canadian Shield, reveling in the abundant biodiversity present there. I am one of the lucky ones to whom being out in the wilds is second nature (pardon the pun) to me, like breathing. It has been my life's mission and joy to share similar places and opportunities with my own children.

I am also a retired elementary school teacher, having taught all grades from Kindergarten to Grade 8. Every September, no matter what

98

grade I was teaching, I made sure I had a self-made terrarium on my desk for the first day. In it would be at least one Monarch, caterpillar or chrysalis or newly emerged butterfly, there to set the tone for the classroom and to welcome my students into the natural world.

Then, depending on the grade level, their first assignment would be to create their own mini-ecosystem, preceded with lots of lessons on how-to and where-to and why-to's. We discussed the necessity of finding out what each "critter" in our terrariums would need to survive for one week and the rule to return the animals and plants back to the same spot from where we had first gathered them for our project. During that week, however, the atmosphere in the classroom was wonderful, as each student had their own wildlife container on their desk for much of the day. They made observations while doing their math or reading; they shared what they had seen happening within each day and they would sadly report if one of their creatures died (or was eaten!). But this exercise made the natural rules of life more real to them. They understood the need for providing the appropriate food, water and shelter that every living thing requires. Little adages like, "An insect lives on its dinner plate" helped them figure out how to satisfy the basic needs of the animals they chose for their own mini-world. Another one was, "Six legs or less is always the best." (I've never really been a fan of spiders.) In addition, there would inevitably be some crickets singing merrily away in a few of the terrariums, before or after class. Very soothing to the teacher! A bit nerve-wracking for the caretaker!

As I always taught in urban areas, a workshop I attended once called Outdoor Education in the Schoolyard was invaluable. From that, we learned to scour the tall grasses caught up in the playground fences, the gardens at the front of the school and even the tarmac for signs of wildlife. I remember one sunny mid-September afternoon, I took my class of fourth-graders out to the front walkway, divided into small groups, each one armed with a magnifying glass or a tripod magnifier.

Everyone chose their own part of the pavement and proceeded to examine the cracks in the concrete for signs of life. Lots of oohs and aahs emanated from the groups scattered about as we all felt like giants peering into rock-strewn chasms. The student I was paired with handed me the magnifier and there I was, butt in the air, nose to the ground when I noticed a pair of shiny black men's shoes edging closer to my peripheral view. Two pairs, actually. I looked up from my ungainly position to see my principal and our area superintendent looking down at me with much amusement. Rather than being embarrassed, I piped up, "Hello, sirs! Would either of you two gentlemen care to take a look! This feels like being in the movie, *A Bug's Life*."

We would play many nature-based games designed to make children more aware of their surroundings and of environmental issues. Most of the games came from a course called Project Wild, and many were specific to certain grade and age levels. Others were applicable to all age groups.

A simple starter was to have the children sit in a circle somewhere on the schoolyard and close their eyes. Keeping one hand in a fist, they would listen for any sounds, natural or man-made. As they heard each new sound, they would raise one finger from the fist and then open their eyes and stand up when all five fingers were raised. A discussion of what sounds were heard would follow. Then, we would sit down again and play Deer's Ears. This involved cupping our hands and placing them first, behind our own ears, and then in front of them. The shape of the hands and the change of position was to mimic the ability of a deer to move its ears around to hear clearly in all directions. The students were amazed in the differences they noted. The concept of Predator/Prey would begin here, as the children realized that good hearing was one of the vital tools that prey animals used to avoid capture.

A very simple game to demonstrate the power of smell was Upwind/Downwind. All you needed was a can of pungent air freshener and a healthy breeze. The children would stand in a line with their backs to the wind. I stood facing them about five yards away and sprayed, but they would smell nothing. Then I would move to the other side of the line, they would turn around facing into the wind and I would repeat. Now, the smell of the air freshener was obvious. From that came, "Stay downwind when you're trying to sneak up on an animal."

The excellent eyesight of predatory birds as well as the prey's use of camouflage was the basis of the next game, a hide-and-seek game simply called Predator and Prey. One child would be chosen as "the eagle" and the rest of the class were "the rabbits." At the signal, the "eagle" would close his eyes and hold onto the school flagpole while the "rabbits" scampered about the school's front campus, looking for places to hide in the shrubbery, the gardens and the building's nooks and crannies. They would hide behind tree trunks, lie down behind flowers and bushes or peek out from the alcove by the building's front door. They were encouraged to consider what colours were in the clothing they wore that day when choosing their hiding spot. A couple of rules were necessary: they could not move once they'd found their spot and they had to be able to see the "eagle" at all times. (That also meant, that as the teacher, I could have all of them in my sight at all times but it impressed upon them the need for prey to remain motionless but watchful when predators were about.)

At the next loudly-given signal, the "eagle" would open her eyes and while touching the flagpole with at least one of her limbs, peer out, looking for "dinner." As each "rabbit" was spotted and pointed out, they had to come out and sit quietly ("Dead bunnies don't make noise.") behind the "eagle" without blocking his view. Once most of the children had been found, I would call for the rest to reveal themselves. A new "eagle" would be chosen and the game would continue. They never tired of this and it became one of our favourite end-of-day activities as we waited for the bell to ring.

These activities all require sizable groups but if we want to get our own kids outside, I turn back to my own childhood. Mom was the one who taught me how to build my first Monarch caterpillar terrarium, and it's a habit I have continued annually for my entire life. It just wouldn't be summer if I didn't do this. Dad taught me to swim and to dive and to fish (and how to be very, very still and quiet while doing the latter!). Mom taught me about wild flowers and they both shared their love and the hard work of gardening with me.

We had a hobby greenhouse out back and I recall many hours out there, as the snow whipped against the glass panes, planting up "flats" of seeds with my father on wintry Sunday afternoons. I learned to mix the soil, to thin the seedlings, to pinch back the sprouting plants to make them bushier and to transplant them into pots. Mom showed me how to arrange them in the garden and how to weed and trim and water and fertilize them. Finally, they cleared a space and gave me my own garden. With their help and interest, it flourished. Years later, long after I'd moved away, Mom came to visit one day and presented me with a bouquet she had gathered from the shambles of my old garden.

My son turned the tables on me one day when he discovered an owl pellet laying on the ground under an old pine tree. For the child who loves puzzles, this is the ultimate one. It's a deliciously gruesome activity for parent and child to pull the pellet apart, pick out tiny bones and bits of fur and then try to reassemble the skeleton of a mouse or shrew that had recently been the owl's dinner.

For the most part, you as the adult have to be willing to "get out there," to find yourself in unfamiliar positions and locales, to laugh at yourself, to get dirty or soaking wet, to discover what you can be passionate about in the great big wild world and share it with your child or the group you are working with. See the wonder and watch them as they see it for the first time too. Augment it with a camera or binoculars or a microscope and you've satisfied their need to hold a device in their hands. Incorporate what they find into artwork or journaling or just plain remembering. Find the joy. Make it real, for you, for them.

Kitty Rogers

Devoted Mom, loyal friend, and mid-western gal through and through.

River Ride

I didn't tell anyone about it. I didn't want to be told that I couldn't do it again. It was so exhilarating, it must have been dangerous. I didn't want to forfeit the chance to go again by sharing too much with too many people.

The adventure started innocently enough. It was such a hot summer's day. My legs were already sticking to my horse's sides as I rode through the field; the mosquitoes were drawn to his damp hay belly, and the horseflies to his sweaty neck. His ears lay back in protest and he shook his head from side to side. I wasn't enjoying their company either. I thought it might be nice to cool him off in the river that ran through the fields, disappeared into the woods and then came out downstream at the bridge into the village.

I'd been in that river before. We'd wade in and stand very still in the shallows while we fished for bluegills and sunfish. I'd felt the tiny pebbles that covered the bottom of the barely tumbling water in the shallow rapids. I'd also slipped on the larger stones and rocks that made crossing in places difficult, but terribly fun, as we'd see who would be the first to fall in and get soaked. I thought we should ride down river a bit and see what it was like.

He didn't mind going in the shallows; the bank wasn't steep. After just a few steps, I nudged him into a trot and giggled at all the water splashing up around us. It was an effort for him to pick up his

104

feet as the water got deeper and he tried to bring them up out of the water with each step. The sparkle of the sunshine on the water spray was magical and cooling. The sound of it all was large and happy.

I did wonder about those larger stones and rocks that were in this part of the river. I did wonder if he'd slip or if he could hurt himself by prancing through the water. But we slowed our pace as the water became deeper and we neared the bend in the river where the woods closed in and hugged the river tight. My concern left me as the air became cooler and the shade darker. The bottom of the river grew muddy and the horse now sunk down with each step as the water rose with each step. Soon he began to breathe a little heavier and exert himself as he pulled each hoof out of the mud and moved us through the river.

The banks rose. There was a large area of cattails to one side and a steep eroded bank on the other. I raised my eyebrows as I took it all in and thought that if we were going to turn back, we should do it now. I'd never been here on the river. I tried to gauge how much farther it was to the bridge and the shallow rapids on either side of it. It couldn't be too far. Let's keep going and see. I asked the horse if he thought he was up to the task and I looked around, thinking I could jump off and get myself over there to the bank if need be.

It was quiet here. It was still. Everything was resting in the heat of the day. The water was deep and the current even. All of a sudden, my shorts were wet. The horse snorted, his feet gave way and there was no lurch forward with the next step, but an entirely new motion as the horse began to swim, straining his neck forward and moving with a rhythm that felt foreign and magical. He was swimming! Had he ever done *that* before? Could he do it? Was it OK that I was on his back? Oh, it was exciting. It was frightening. I couldn't believe it. I was impressed with the river's depth and power. I felt such respect for horse.

The horse seemed to swim on and on, but it couldn't have been too long. I was caught in a moment of marvel and awe on my horse in the river in the woods. It filled me. I was relieved when he found his footing again. Was he? We were both confident now as he walked through water that was growing shallower and shallower. We were accomplished as we stepped into the tumbling rapids and he picked up the pace of his own accord and trotted out of the river into the meadow right before the bridge. I almost slipped from his back as he shook the water from his coat and took off running through the meadow towards home.

Did we go there again? I seem to remember going down river with him a second time, but I may be mistaken. It's the first time that I remember so well. I feel how it moved me over and over again and I wonder what he thought of it.

Kirsty Stevenson

Kirsty Stevenson left her urban lifestyle in 1999 and has never looked back. She lives at the base of a ski hill and, in winter, spends as much time as possible on the slopes – one of her greatest passions is downhill skiing. Her winter days are defined by skiing and her summer days include hiking and biking on the Niagara Escarpment and countless hours spent in and around Georgian Bay, located only minutes from her home.

Her enthusiasm for everything outdoors extends to her volunteer life as well. In 2007 she founded the Georgian Bay Titans RFC, the only rugby club in the area where she lives, and continues to act as president.

Kirsty has been an entrepreneur for her entire business career, starting the first landscape lighting company in Canada and moving on to other endeavours including inventing and manufacturing Bling Snaps, a pin-type decorative accessory, and, most recently, launching KIRSTO to provide advice to small business. Her love of the outdoors weaves its way through the fabric of her life each and every day.

I LOVE TO SKI

I love to ski.

I really love to ski

I really really love to ski…. People learn that almost as soon as they meet me because skiing is frequently on my mind regardless of the season. If I'm asked for a photo, it's hard to find one without my ski helmet and goggles.

Every year when the leaves begin to make their way from the lush green of summer to the auburn tones of fall I get butterflies in my stomach because I know that snow will soon be on its way. I tell myself that this year it will be different, this year I won't be the crazed skier woman, chasing the powder after every snowfall, getting in as many days as possible and ticking them off on my skiing calendar, driving in the blinding snow to get fresh tracks at the resort next door when my home club is not open.

It's easy to be ski-crazy when you live across the street from a chairlift. It's not quite ski-in ski-out because there is a road in the way, but it's pretty good.

My big decision each morning is whether to put my skis on and glide down to one chairlift or to continue hiking and go up, perhaps 100 yards, to the other chairlift. It's a very tough decision.

I do not live in a postcard-perfect mountain town, but reside at the bottom of the Niagara Escarpment, one of the UNESCO'S World Biosphere Reserves. It's a magnificent ancient geological feature, formed during the last Ice Age when the ice receded.

The Escarpment is 1000 miles total in length and approximately 750 feet elevation where I'm located. A mile behind my house lies Georgian Bay, an off-shoot of Lake Huron and one of the most beautiful bodies of fresh water in the world. In the winter I ski; in the summer I have the luxury of being a two-minute drive from the beach.

My love for skiing began as a small child when I was put on skis shortly after I learned to walk. Dad and I would get dressed, ready to march across the road to the rope tow. More often than not he would carry me up the little hill because the snow was usually deeper than I was tall. We'd arrive at the rope tow and he'd place me in between his legs, grab on to the rope, and off we'd go. It didn't take long before I was on my own.

I loved to ski with my Dad. He was an old-fashioned beautiful skier, feet planted firmly together, swooshing down the slopes with incredible grace and style. By the time I was a teenager he was chasing me down the hills, yelling loudly, "Turn, dammit, turn!!!" I still love to ski really fast.

I grew up in downtown Toronto, but my father insisted that we were a skiing family so we trekked two hours up the highway every winter weekend. Even after my parents divorced my mother continued the tradition. It was certainly not because she loved to ski – Mom never really progressed further than the snowplow – but because she thought it was an important ritual to continue.

I seldom missed a weekend of skiing my entire life. Even through university, starting my career, getting married and having two children, I continued to make the journey north to ski each weekend.

Since moving to the country to live full time I have skied over 100 days in the winter season many times. It's hard to believe this is even possible, but I get up each morning, put on my ski gear and head out, if even for an hour or two. The locals call it the "power hour", on the chairlift as soon as it opens, ski like mad for one to two hours, and then off to put in a full day at work.

I am self-employed so have the flexibility to time-shift my day to permit me to ski in the mornings. If something gets in the way of my morning "fix" I can go night-skiing at the resort just south of where I live.

Although our wee little hill is not nearly as tall as mountains found elsewhere, I manage to get in as many or more days and vertical feet as most keen skiers anywhere in the world. I will ski in any weather, cold or really cold, dry snow or wet, windy or rainy, it does not matter. I live in Grey County and in February it's true to its name. Grey days followed by grey days, but I am not deterred. The snow still feels the same beneath my skis.

Once I leave the house my worldly concerns fall away and it's only me and the hill, me and the snow, me and the sky, trees, birds and animals. Nothing else exists. I often close my eyes on the chairlift and listen to the sounds of winter - the rush of the wind through the evergreens, the scraping of skis on ice, the laughter of children as they tumble down the hills, and the peace of a world covered in snow.

Living across from the hill I've come to understand the sound of the seasons as much as the look and smell of them. Each fall, after the leaves have gone, the trees begin to moan. The wind starts at Lake Huron, about 60 miles away, and picks up speed as it dashes over the flat landscape, only to roar down the Escarpment to where I live.

The area between the ski runs is covered by hardwood trees with a few evergreens interspersed. The barren trees sway and dance together in the wind moaning and crying for their lost leaves. It's truly an awe-inspiring sound. One day the snow falls and the world becomes silent. The trees stop lamenting the loss of their leaves and acquiesce to their winter blanket.

I am often overcome with wonderment as I stand at the hilltop, drinking in the turquoise and indigo hues of the water, reveling in the beauty of the land and water scapes spread at my feet. There are very few ski resorts that have a view over any body of water and the majesty of this view informs each day. It becomes part of the experience – the water is always there, the weather molds and shapes itself over the slate grey canvas into winter storms in their entire splendor. I am a fortunate witness.

I am ready, prepared for flight. I edge forward, tilting my body out over the steep pitch, knowing that I must commit, must lean way out to make that first pole plant. Once I'm committed, my body soars.

I rise up to make the first turn, feel my skis bite into the snow, and then disappear into a reverie of bliss. I float from turn to turn, feeling the hill beneath my skis, joy and wonder, harmony and heaven manifesting in every turn.

People often comment on what a smooth and flowing skier I am. It's because I am listening to the hill, letting the slope tell me how to ski it, working with the shape of the incline, letting gravity carry me to the bottom, letting joy carry me away.

I finish the track with love and grace in my heart, ready to do it all again. And again. And again.

I try to enjoy each run without judgment of how well I skied. This is not to say that I haven't had my share of crashes and burns, frights and failures, but most days I finish with a huge smile on my face.

I flow with the hill, the snow, the weather, and the great outdoors until the big melt, usually sometime in late March or early April. During the winter the out-of-doors is my domain. It is there I want to be, not cooped up inside.

Each year when approaching my last run, I stand at the crest of the escarpment and absorb the view for the last time for the season. I know I will be returning soon to hike, but I say so long for the time being. I give thanks to the ski-gods for keeping me safe for yet another year and wish goodness upon all of the creatures who take over the hills when I and the other skiers depart.

My wish is for all people to know a love of the outdoors that so defines and inspires and brings such immeasurable joy.

One day, a number of years ago, we had a huge dump of lovely fresh powder. I skied for about an hour and, by then, most of the "freshie" had been carved up by me and the other powder seekers. I was skiing down a nice steep run and noticed a small cut-out on skier's right. I found a stash of untracked, untouched flawless powder. It was completely silent in my little corner; I heard nothing but the soft swish as I stole through the newly fallen snow. It was no more than five turns, but I was completely fulfilled.

I reached the bottom and felt my heart swelling inside my chest, knowing that I had just experienced perfection, if that was at all possible, and that life was so good it was time to go home and just be present with the joy in my heart.

But, as always, the crazy skier woman emerged and I hopped on the chairlift, ready for the next run.

Nick Chedli Carter

Born and raised in Washington, D.C., Nick is a 2008 graduate of the University of Vermont and continues to live and work in the Burlington area as a public affairs specialist for a health care organization. Stuck most days in his office or at the Vermont Statehouse, he can often be found pursuing some form of outdoor activity most weekends and afternoons, particularly snowboarding in the winter, hiking and biking in the spring and summer. In addition to writing, he enjoys photography and produces local radio and public access television programming.

Revolution Summer

To start off I should make it clear that in NO way do I consider myself an 'outdoorsman' or 'outdoor enthusiast' or whatever term is used these days to highlight one's interest in being outside. I've been drawn to the outdoors much like a moth to a flame (though for me the results are overwhelmingly positive). I find this desire to be absolutely inherent to my existence and identity but I don't consider that to be exceptional – humans need to be outside!

The days when I'm unable to spend time outdoors I almost feel like I'm committing a crime against humanity and have deprived my soul of an essential nutrient. Okay, maybe that's a little too dramatic but being outdoors does indeed jump-start my proverbial life force in many ways. Whether it's biking on road or off, kayaking down a rapid, swimming in a lake, hiking up/down a mountain or snowboarding in the winter, being outside is a true necessity for me and positively impacts not just my physical well-being but very much my emotional and spiritual development.

This pro-outdoors mindset was likely cultivated by my fortunate summer experiences spent in a small town in Central Vermont. Every year, usually around late June, my sister, mom and I would embark on a twelve-hour Amtrak ride from Union Station in Washington D.C. up to the Green Mountain majesty that is the state of Vermont. The ride was long and boring, but was a welcome departure from urban reality. I'll never forget how crisp and refreshing the air was every time we stepped off the train at the one-room Montpelier train station. My dad would drive up with the bikes, junk and the dog and the proceeding next couple of months were always a time of pure happiness and filled with many, many days outside and occasional nights by a fire.

Those summers spent in a log cabin at the end of a long, beautiful dirt road provided the perfect playground for a young boy and his bike. The road, conveniently named Rec Field Road, has the fish aplenty Winooski River running alongside it and that first evening drive up to the cabin was always exciting for I knew I'd be waking up to days of fun and adventure. (Also, it was so dark and quiet compared to back home!)

Unlike our townhouse in D.C., the only neighbor was an organic vegetable farm and the family who ran it conveniently had a son my age, Jacob. A typical day consisted of getting on my bike in the morning and seeing what Jacob and his friend in town, Andy, were up to. The possibilities were endless and unless it was raining, there was no doubt we'd be experiencing the profound glory that is summer in a place like Central Vermont. One day might entail a day's long forage in the woods, with no particular agenda or goal other than to check out a spot we'd never been to before. Another day might be a pick-up baseball game at the rec field, fishing in the river, hiking with Jacob's mom or seeing how far our bikes could get us on the abandoned railroad bed behind the house. Sometimes I'd see my friend Spencer in

Calais and spend hours on crystal clear Mirror Lake. Days were unstructured, and as long as we checked in at home by dinner, we were pretty much on our own, which suited us just fine.

The differences between myself and my summer friends were subtle compared to our unified desire for adventure and freedom. I'll never forget when Andy's older brother was talking about their family's camp and I said, "Oh, what's it called? I went to a summer camp too." Andy quickly informed my city ass about the real definition of camps as being an informal getaway for folks before an all-out water gun war broke out between us and the other kids.

Jacob's family runs an organic vegetable farm next to our cabin and spending time over there was like being in a utopia of vegetables and cool looking farm equipment. "So this is where food comes from," I remember thinking to myself. "Not just from Safeway!" My sister and I would help out with harvesting and tasks like moving irrigation pipes and she even went on to study agriculture at Cornell as a direct result of spending time on that farm. Getting to see, touch and feel what goes into growing food has been key to my understanding of how and what to eat, and how important local food systems are to small communities.

My dad recently dug up a copy of an old local paper where a ten-year-old me is quoted as saying "Vermont life's the life for me." It was part of a story on summer visitors to the state and what I'm referring to in the article is a life of being able to really spend time outdoors; not having to drive hours to go for a bike ride or take a swim, not having to worry what to do for fun but rather being able to embrace life and its uncertainties and being comfortable with the day's plan being to have no plan at all.

Coming back to D.C. in the fall was always resented by my entire family. It wasn't just going back to school and work but knowing that things just aren't as easy to simply 'be' outside and enjoy nothing more than the stars in the sky and the sound of frogs and crickets in the air. Most of us like summer regardless of where we are but that time at the end of Rec Field Road represented to us how life could be and the rest of the year was just sort of an 'in-between' time.

Don't get me wrong; I maximized my urban outdoor experience as a skateboarder, little leaguer, back alley basketball player and generally mischievous (or should I say 'curious') adolescent. Spending time outside in the urban jungles has its own special enjoyment and adventure but it isn't quite the same as being able to jump into a clean, flowing river – bathing suits and pool memberships be damned!

My love of the outdoors has manifested itself in many forms and I've participated in just about any of the '-ing' activities you can think of. Now as a twenty-seven-year-old living in Vermont, I attribute much of my desire and contentment to be in a rural state as a direct result of those summers. I'm still very good friends with Jacob and Spencer and my family still makes the trip up every summer. We all look forward to the time together in and around the cabin, and know that so much of our relationships with each other and ourselves has been impacted by that time spent outside.

Pauline Loewenhardt

Pauline is an outdoor enthusiast living in the Midwest. Contracting polio as a child did not slow her down. She has hiked, gardened, kayaked, and skied in many parts of this country and in Europe. She is also a singer.

WHY I LOVE TO BE OUTDOORS

A few days ago I kayaked on Mill Lake with my friend, Ellie. It was a perfect day – sunny, not too hot, light breeze. We are a great pair...she is 82 years old and needs a little help getting out of her Pokeboat. I am 79 and need a hand to steady the boat as I get in my kayak. Once we are pushed off, we lazily circle the lake. She remembers every bird she sees or hears, a dedicated birder. I like searching the water and land for turtles, snakes and other wildlife and identifying plants. We bring a lunch and find a quiet spot to eat. We sometimes have the whole lake to ourselves. Paddling in my kayak on a lake or river is my most pleasurable activity of the paddling seasons. I love it intensely and never pass up an opportunity to go kayaking.

Later that day we visited the Gerald Eddy Discovery Center near Chelsea, Michigan, and after exploring the displays in the center, sat for a long time on their large observation deck. Trees all around us bustled with bird activity. It was heaven on earth right there for me. Any activity that takes me outdoors is right up there at the top of my list of pleasures. Just sitting on my little patio in the evening is absolutely meditative and relaxing. I sit in my old wooden rocker and watch the birds at my feeders and in the trees and feel grateful for all my blessings. The older I get, the more intense the pleasure of being in nature. I'm still not sure how my love of nature and the outdoors developed.

My days of playing outdoors as a child came to an abrupt halt in 1944 when, at the age of ten years, I had polio. I spent six weeks in isolation at Herman Kiefer Hospital in Detroit, Michigan, and then eight months at a rehabilitation center in Mount Clemens. There were very few opportunities to be outside. Before this event, which would profoundly change my life, my brothers, sister and I played outside every day. There was an empty field at the end of our block where we played games and built forts. As we got older, we walked a few blocks to Oakman Boulevard to the Wonder Bread Bakery. Behind this building, that still stands today, was a creek. We loved playing there and brought home tadpoles in a bucket. We really thought we could grow the tadpoles into frogs on our back porch and were sad when they all died.

A big event of my childhood was a trip to Palmer Park in Detroit, Michigan. Because of the war, these trips did not occur often. The park was wilderness as far as I was concerned. I remember the little stone bridge where the four of us posed for a picture taken by my Dad with our Brownie camera. We are smiling happily. I still remember the joy of eating a meal outdoors at a picnic table. Gasoline was rationed during WWII and those were the years of my childhood. There were a few trips to Toledo to visit relatives. We ate our meals at long tables set up under tall trees. These visits stand out in my memory. Most of my relatives lived in Germany. It was so good to be with family, even though they were distant cousins living in Toledo, Ohio.

My first experience of "country living" came when I was in college. My good friend, Joanne, was from a farm near Caseville up in the "thumb" of Michigan. I spent weekends with her and met her parents and family. I will always remember delicious meals of fresh picked corn on the cob, sliced fresh tomatoes, and other good things from their garden. I can't forget the homemade bread her Mom baked. The big table in the kitchen was dominated by loud laughter and conversation of her big Dad and brothers. However, the country roads terrified me. No traffic signals. Few stop signs and absolute zero visibility because of the high corn rows that came to the edges of the roads. I knew then that I was a city kid, but there was a part of me that always wanted to live in the country.

Somehow, in spite of the polio, which fortunately left me with only a slight limp due to paralysis of my left foot and ankle, I learned to downhill ski. I was never very skilled at it but loved the sport and being outside in winter. The thrill of standing at the top of a hill and then sliding down, sometimes ending in a heap, was absolute joy.

By then I had graduated from college and was working as a nurse. My friends and I managed to take trips to Caberfae, a ski resort near Cadillac, Michigan. In later years I learned to cross-country ski and enjoyed that just as much and found it less stressful. Now I have a pair of snowshoes that allow me to be out in the winter. Of course the snowy winters are now more rare, but one day last winter I was able to snowshoe right out of my driveway to the large expanse of open fields and woods across the street that are part of the Leslie Science Center.

I married in 1957 and so a whole new era began. I had three kids and learned to garden. We lived in a house with a huge backyard on the west side of Detroit. From my kitchen window, I could see a huge willow tree at the far end of the yard. I called it my green curtain and loved watching it move with the wind. Next door lived a retired gentleman who had a beautiful garden which I envied. Our yard was quite barren except for grass. We became friends and he began handing me plants over the fence and would carefully tell me where to plant them. I particularly remember the large dinner-plate-size dahlias. They were gorgeous. I dug them up in the fall and hung them from the rafters in the basement and then replanted them the following spring when they came back to life. They continued to bloom for all the years we lived there. My love of gardening is one of the mainstays of my life. Wherever I find myself living, whether a big house or small condo, I have to have a place where I can dig in the dirt and plant flowers and vegetables.

My most intricate garden took shape when I decided to attract butterflies and birds in the late 80s. I dug up the front lawn of our house in Tampa, Florida, and planted a butterfly garden. Monarchs came to visit along with many other varieties. I have photos of all the Monarch's stages of development from egg to larvae eating the leaves of milkweed to chrysalis and finally to a butterfly. For a Midwesterner, gardening in Florida was a challenge at first. It meant learning a whole new lexicon of plants, gardening rules, seasons and living with strange critters I had never encountered before. Some, like the little lizards that found their way into the house, were easy to live with. When my cat brought in a little snake, I drew the line there. Snakes needed to be outside. They liked my butterfly garden as the ground cover of jasmine provided shade and a place to hide. I treasure a certificate from the city of Tampa awarded to households that provide wildlife habitat and conserve water. My yard also became certified by the National Wildlife Federation as a wildlife habitat.

I also became involved with our Seminole Heights Neighborhood Association and wrote articles for the newsletter about gardening and helped plan events. We lived very close to the Hillsborough River, which ran through Tampa. Walks at the river were an everyday occurrence since I had a companion dog at that time. Neighborhood events also took place at the park on the river. There was an abundance of wildlife in the park. I remember once parking my bike under a palm tree after a ride and feeling bits of something fishy falling from the sky. Looking up, I saw a bald eagle in the tree, eating a fish. Another time, Charlie stopped on the bank of the river and barked anxiously. I looked down and there was a mother manatee with her calf circling just under the water.

Gradually I acquired a large collection of outdoor potted plants. The nice thing about sub-tropical living is that they can live outside all year round. Except, of course, for the times when there are hurricanes approaching. Then we had a jungle inside the house as we brought in more than fifty potted plants, some that required two people to lift and carry. When it came time to move out of state, I had a party and guests were encouraged to take home a potted plant. I am still in touch with friends who have some of my plants.

Memorable scenes flash across my mind from years ago. A visit to Hawaii in 1971 to visit my youngest brother. We snorkeled in Hanauma Bay Nature Preserve. It was breathtaking to be floating in the Pacific Ocean watching the brightly colored sea life beneath me. We also spent a day deep-sea fishing. I couldn't believe I had a large sailfish on my line. I was happy he got away after a lengthy struggle.

On a later trip, after my brother and his wife moved to the big island of Hawaii, we walked in the woods near his house on the side of the extinct volcano, Mauna Kea. On their five-acre property, they raise a few sheep to keep the grass "mowed." They grow pineapple and palm trees as well as other tropical plants. My guess is that Joe and I inherited our love of nature and the outdoors from our mother. He rises at 5:00 a.m. every day and takes a walk through the woods with their dogs. Though, as children, we lived in a big city, we always had a backyard garden and Mama canned fruits and vegetables and made wonderful peach jam from a tree in our yard. She grew up in a small town in Germany and had experience with gardening.

I've hiked in forests and woods in many states, all of them memorable. The hushed stillness of walking among the trees holds a special place in my heart. I've walked in the state of Washington on the rugged beach of the Olympic Peninsula and up Hurricane Ridge, also on the peninsula. I've hiked Blood Mountain in Georgia near the Appalachian Trail. I've walked in Alaska, Wisconsin, Minnesota, Michigan (both upper and lower peninsulas), Colorado – where my daughter Morgan lives, California, Arizona, New Mexico and Florida. As the years pass, I am walking more slowly and now use a forearm crutch for balance. But I continue to walk. The arboretum here in Ann Arbor, Michigan, is a favorite place to walk, especially when the peonies are in bloom.

Last summer, on a trip with my ten-year-old grandson, Ryan and his mother, Linda, we visited Chautauqua, in New York State. Ryan's first request when we arrived was a walk to the creek. It took a long time to get to the creek and required some climbing up and down rocky paths, but it was delightful. He waded in the creek and built stone cairns. It was the joyful highlight of my day. I have made several trips to Europe, in particular, to the Netherlands where I have relatives. It is customary there to plan a walk outdoors as part of every special occasion, even weddings. I've walked in woods and in fields of Scotland, the Lake District of England, and many places in the Netherlands. I also spent three days walking around Paris. Not nature, per se, but nevertheless, very memorable. A precious memory of my first trip to Dalfsen, the small village where my cousin Louise lives with her husband, is riding the heavy Dutch bikes with a big basket in front. In 1997, on my first trip, we went for several wonderful bicycle rides through the countryside. A 12-foot-wide lane is provided, well away from the roadway, where people walk, ride bicycles, roller blade and even ride motor scooters. It seems a very civilized way to encourage people to be outdoors. The lane is divided in half and walkers are on one side and those with wheels are on the other.

I learned to ride a bicycle rather later than most children. I was about twelve when I finally had a bike and could gather up the courage to try it. Once I learned however, it became a favorite pastime. I still have a little folding bike in my garage. However, I have not ridden it in a couple of years. There are too many hills in my current neighborhood. I did enjoy riding it around Geddes Lake, the condo complex where I lived a few years ago. The complex was set on 65 acres of beautiful rolling hills with three spring-fed lakes. It was home to many forms of wildlife including ducks, trumpeter swans, birds and small mammals. I was part of the Lakes and Grounds committee and initiated plans to establish a rain garden in the complex. I did enjoy living there and would still be there except for the fact that all the condos are two stories. I can no longer handle climbing stairs very well.

I moved to Ann Arbor, Michigan, in 2003. For the first ten years that I lived here I was active on the Huron River Watershed Council. I participated in the semi-annual river round-ups in which teams of volunteers go out to stream sites to collect macro invertebrates. These are then counted and provide clues as to the health of the streams flowing into the Huron River. It is nationally recognized as the longest running river research project in the country. I still volunteer occasionally but am not able to go out to the stream sites.

My love of nature, the environment and earth and all its creatures has found its fullest expression in my membership with a group of women singers. We call ourselves The Gaia Women of the Great Lakes Basin. We are a group of about 40 women from two countries, Canada and the United States. The waters of the Detroit River draw us together rather than divide us. Most of us live in Metro Detroit, Ann Arbor or Windsor, Ontario, though several come from as far away as Toronto. We meet monthly for a full day of singing, reflection and activism. We sing love songs to earth and send a message of hope and healing for our bio-region and the planet. We sing the music of Carolyn McDade, a unique activist and songwriter of many years. Her music explores the deep connection between earth and those who inhabit this planet. We lend our voices to different events such as a recent outdoor church service in Northport, Michigan, on the

Leelanau Peninsula that celebrated a yearlong collaboration between church members and members of a Native American tribe living nearby. Later that day the tribe members welcomed all to a water walk that celebrated water.

It is becoming more and more evident that caring for the earth is no longer something that only a few people can or should do. We all must, each one of us, put our heart and soul into the struggle to save her for future generations. Although I said in the beginning of this essay that I was not sure how my love of the outdoors and nature developed, I see now that it has been there all along from my earliest childhood. It has taken different forms over the years and now finds its expression in my simple everyday activities of feeding the birds, caring for a little garden of mostly native plants, living lightly on Gaia and singing love songs to her.

Peggy Howard

Peggy Howard lives in Berlin, Vermont, with her husband Geoff, whom she married 25 years ago. She is a proud mother of Ashley, who is a middle school teacher. She has been happily employed as a rehabilitation counselor for the past 29 years and works with people who are blind and visually impaired. She enjoys spending every free moment at the ocean.

DIGGING, BEACHING, AND SPENDING TIME WITH THOSE I LOVE

It turns out I have always enjoyed digging in the dirt. The earliest memory I have of this involves my older brother. He is such a card, so funny and imaginative. Any attention he gave me was very much enjoyed. I wonder if he knew. He is nine years older than me and boy did I look up to him when I was a kid. He had the greatest ideas for fun.

We had an unusual backyard when I was a little girl. There was a section that was dug out when the house was built but never covered up. It exposed a huge sand hill that lead up to the woods. The sand was perfect. I think I was about five years old when my brother, Mr. Ingenious, decided to turn the hill into a super neighborhood. Tennis balls were used as the cars and they could roll through the hand dug valleys and tunnels. We would start at the top of the hill and let the balls roll down through our maze of streets and handmade villages. We had fake trees made from branches of trees and garden gates of stones. Blocks of wood from my dad's shop made great houses and buildings.

Hours were spent building this special place. It was so much fun to stand on the top of the hill, let the ball go and watch where it would travel. It would wind back and forth through the hand built roads. Our goals was to make sure the turns and dips were structured just right so the ball could make it to the bottom of the hill. The turns had to be deep so the ball would not fall out of the track. That was our goal and thrilling when we were successful. As we progressed we had more than one route the ball could travel down. We would let two and three balls go at the same time, watching as they would miss hitting at the different intersections. We built tunnels and bridges, watching one ball roll under the bridge while another rolled over. I spent hours playing on the hill, even after my brother moved on to other things to do during the day.

One night in particular, I remember my mom calling me in for supper. It was getting darker but I could not pull myself away from this magical place. "Please can I stay out just a little longer?" It was a memorable time as my mom said, "Ok," and left me to play long after the rest of the family ate supper. It was one of those special nights when the air had a warm breeze. I was busy with my imagination until I got tired and hungry and went in on my own.

Summer days are warm on Long Island and the woods behind the house were a great place to relax in the shade. On top of the hill was a huge tree with four trunks growing up from the earth. It was a perfect tree house. We hammered steps and hung signs to keep the neighborhood kids away. Paths were dug to resemble roads that were lined with rocks. We made a little fire pit and my mom would let us build small fires to cook our hot dog lunch. I became a great fire builder. It was fun to pretend we lived up there and we tried our best to make it our little house during the day. We were always changing what we hung on the tree. Old pieces of wood made shelves and signs. One time we even hung curtains from some old material. The tree was wonderful and stood up tall and stunning to whatever we did.

My two older sisters also had some good ideas about how to have fun. We had a ritual on warm summer nights when my parents would go out. We would wait until the sky was very dark and the stars were bright. We all had our jobs to do to get ready for our adventure. We gathered a blanket to lie on, hot tea, cups and saltine crackers with grape jelly. This was carefully set up on our front lawn. After our snack we would gaze up at the stars and make up stories. The best part of the night was not getting caught by our parents. Every time we saw headlights coming up the street we had to get into drill mode. We needed to pick everything up and run around the back of the house to the door. When inside we had to run and duck under every window, jump into bed, pull up the covers and pretend we were sleeping. We did this many times until my parents eventually returned home. We never got caught! (I wonder if they ever knew what we were up to.)

My younger brother loved following the weather. The bigger the storm the more excited he was. I can remember being in my room and hearing him practice, "This is your meteorologist with the latest weather report." I think he was recording his voice on a tape recorder. Snowstorms on Long Island are rough and wet. When outside you can feel the tiny pieces of ice hitting against your face. This may sound hard to believe, but we loved it. It usually meant we were stranded at home and if we were lucky we would lose electricity, requiring the family to sleep around the fireplace in the living room. Most memorable was the blizzard of 1978! I remember digging out. I think we had about two feet of snow. Instead of a direct path to the driveway, my brother and I decided to make a maze. My parents didn't appreciate this unusual idea but we had a blast!

Growing up by the beach gave me many opportunities to play in the sand. I loved and still do love the feeling of suntan lotion and sand all over me. Many summer days were spent at our little neighborhood beach. Low tide was great for building towns with rivers and valleys. Sitting by the tides letting the water splash in my face and cooling in the salt water are some of my favorite things. After a cool swim, lying on the hot sand worked well to get rid of the chill.

I am blessed to have great friends who also enjoy the ocean and every year we make our annual trek to a beautiful Cape Cod beach. We have been going for 25 years. We pack up our gear and families and head to our little rented cottage for a week of boogie board surfing in the crashing waves. My husband wraps himself up in suntan lotion and towels under the umbrella. One year we had the girls lie in the sand while we shaped the earth around them into mermaids. They were beautiful! Many wonderful memories have been made during these trips. Racing to sunset beach after supper, fires on the beach at night, whale watch adventures and a good book with my toes digging in the sand are some of the best things.

We have an event that takes place with an annual visit with great friends from out of state. When they are here we build the luge run. Everyone is involved with digging, planning, piling snow, fixing walls and sliding. The course has many twists, dips and turns. Just before our friends arrive I head out to the store to replace the tubes. They only last one year. By the end of the day we usually have a slippery, very fast slide. The lights get pointed on the luge and the screaming begins. Sometimes bodies fly out over the borders and we need to strengthen the wall. Sometimes people are going so fast they speed out of the track and over my neighbor's freshly shoveled driveway, across their lawn and down the street. These events usually involve a fire by the hot tub, a huge dinner and many laughs with good memories. We are probably not the best neighbors this one weekend per year as we can get a little loud. You have to be brave to go down the hill as you need to relax and let the tube take you in the right direction. It is when you try to direct your path that you can get into trouble. As scary as it is I have not chickened out yet!

I still enjoy digging. I love to dig in the dirt and make a new garden bed, creating different designs, always moving flowers around. Working late into the evening on a warm summer night is appealing. Relaxing with a late dinner and sitting by the fire pit sipping on a cup of tea is a great way to end the day. My bones may feel a little sore but I am satisfied that I created something new.

Sean McNamara

Sean McNamara is an artist and writer living in the San Juan Mountains of southwestern Colorado. He has never met an ocean, lake, river, forest, mountain or canyon he doesn't love. His most prized possessions are his guitar, his bicycle, his skis and his surfboard.

THE WILD WEST IN FOUR PARTS

Riding for a Reason

Once in a while, on summer weekends, there arises a hankering that can't be resisted. I don cycling togs, ready my bike and tell my sweetheart: "I'll be back in a few hours, honey; just going for a little spin of the pedals."

"Where are you going?"

"Oh, I'm not exactly sure; I'm going on a … um, *fitness* ride."

She knows better.

There are three directions in which I might find what I'm looking for. The first, north to town, is discarded out of hand, because it is too much like going to work. A beautiful commute, yes, past Dead Man's Corner, big mountains to the west, across a rolling mesa of lupine and aster, swooping at high speed around Coor's Corner at the top of Lawson Hill, but the big city is avoided, a behaviorally conditioned response.

The second choice, south on the highway over the pass to Rocko, is taken when motivation is but medium: it's an easy ride on smooth pavement once the dirt road of the valley is left behind, and I know that I can find what I'm looking for at the gas station at the south end of town in Rocko. There's also a comfortable wooden bench there on which to relax, under the porch roof in the shade, before the return journey.

When the whole afternoon is available, however, and favorable weather, the third choice, east over the Jeep pass, then down the highway to Snowmobile usually rules the day. While it is true that this route takes a little longer and requires more effort, the reward is all the sweeter.

And the reward? Simple and straightforward: root beer.

We are not allowed to keep soda pop in the house, for my wife is far wiser than me in all regards and knows that I would just drink it. Having proclaimed long ago that she didn't sign up for a toothless old man when she married, a ban on sugary drinks was put into place and I was thrust into the curious position of getting into more trouble for drinking a soda pop than a beer.

Who remembers their first Halloween? Who remembers the resultant white sugar jet fuel 1000 mile-an-hour flaming-rocket half-crazed running-in-circles joy ride? Who can forget? All attempts at inebriation in ensuing decades have been, in comparison, feeble.

Perhaps it is for a small reminder of this innocent joy that root beer is craved. Maybe it just tastes good. More likely, though, the attraction lies in the fact that it is forbidden fruit; this is one of the funny ways the mind works.

Up the pass it is then, on a mission of sinful nature, past the beaver ponds and into the great aspen stands, an understory of gentian and blue geranium waving softly. The rains have come and brought with them biting black flies by the horde, the escape of their bite motivation enough on the first steep pitches to keep pedaling. You sweat rivers.

Past treeline a light breeze keeps the flies at bay, but the challenge is now embraced, a pursuit rather than flight, and a little light suffering will see you to the top of the pass, the world spread before you, red-streaked peaks waltzing to the horizon. A glide down the ribbon of road, contouring in and out of drainages, trunks of old-growth spruce tossed like matchsticks on the facing wall of the valley by massive avalanches in the not-too-distant past, brings you to the highway and its velvet asphalt S-turns into Snowmobile.

Here, without further ado, you take a seat on the curb in front of the grocery store and before you know it you're enjoying the ice cream headache from guzzling a tall, frosty root beer non-stop, bubbles up the nose, tears in the eyes, an animal act over which there is precious little control. Back on the bike then, burping, because your repast is at this point only half-earned.

The ride back up the highway and pass affords opportunity to take in what you missed on the headlong rush for the demon root beer: head-high cutbanks of mud and cobbles from a recent flash flood in a side creek; roadkill in the form of pancaked snakes and fly catchers, ferrets and flickers; a chipmunk darting for the cover of a roadside dandelion; mighty anvils of fleece building on the ridgelines above; assorted nuts and bolts shed from passing Jeeps in the dirt; ski tracks in the snow at the top of the pass, white snakes through windblown red dirt of the desert, turns like signatures: you can tell who made them by their shape and how they're stacked.

In the notch at the top of the pass there is a feeling of peacefulness, stands of fir and pine climbing the hillsides in broad, deep green strokes, adjacent scree glowing yellow, homes nestled below. The main exertion is done, the madness is over, but you have to admit in the end that somehow, in the relative heat of summertime, with the sweat pouring down, nothing satisfies – maybe the addition of some salty potato chips – quite like an ice cold root beer.

Uncle in the Doghouse

As one heads south on the Big Spring Canyon Trail from the Squaw Flat campground in the Needles District of Canyonlands National Park, the turnoff for Elephant Canyon can be easy to miss, if one is engrossed in conversation and has a nose on the trail instead of looking up.

By the time I realized we'd missed our turn, we were well on our way to the top of Big Spring, ascending from the creekbed up a series of slickrock ledges. Our goal for the day was the Joint Trail across the southern edge of Chesler Park, the shortest route being via Elephant.

We went with Plan B: continue to the top of Big Spring to Squaw Canyon and from there head west, reaching Chesler by traversing the upper drainages of Elephant. The trail, new territory, was nothing short of spectacular: taking advantage of weaknesses in the walls dividing the drainages, it wound a highly improbable course with many wonderful contortions through serpentine arroyos and jumbled hoodoos.

It followed benches along the base of monumental banded sandstone spires – the acclaimed Needles – in and out of amphitheaters that were separate worlds from each other. Steel ladders bolted to the rock provided passage over saddles dividing the tops of the canyons. At one point the route afforded passage through a long tunnel, the air cool and liquid, large juniper logs jammed into the crack in the floor for steps. Upon emerging at the far end, descent from the exit ledge was achieved with a notched log for a staircase.

Our companions were swallows borne by a light breeze whispering along the rust and bone slopes, and whiptails that scurried at our approach to the shadows beneath yucca and prickly pear. The late-April day was perfect: blue sky, wispy clouds, the sun hot but not stinking hot, a day tailor-made for hiking in the desert.

Snatches of German could be heard from other hikers. We caught up with a young Danish fellow who hiked solo, carrying a gallon of water in one hand. His expression was child-like and full of wonder: "This place is incredible; there is nothing like it anywhere!" As we bid him farewell and continued on the dusty trail, we realized: he was right.

The miles piled up, and eventually we approached a gap in the mighty pillars that marked the portal to Chesler Park. After a short climb we entered the inner sanctum, a flat, grassy plain fenced in by fins and spires, a hidden garden, a secret world.

Here, at the junction of the Joint Trail, in the shade of a piñon in a sandy draw, I suggested to my niece and hiking partner Robyn that we might be well advised to forego the Joints and start making our way back. I'd noticed, but didn't mention, that the last couple of miles she'd been lagging further and further behind on the trail, her confident stride taken over gradually by an unsteady gait.

She protested: "But I wanna see the Joints!"

My inner Mean Uncle came out: "Honey, it ain't happening. We have a long way to go. Eat this bagel and apple and drink some water. Time to cowgirl up."

The call was made none too soon, for as we made our way across Chesler, Robyn's pace slowed further. I reminded her of the grilled ranchhand steak with potatoes and wild asparagus we'd had for dinner the night before to bolster ourselves for this very hike, but she grew despondent. She sighed, "I guess I just don't have it today. Is there any way we can get a ride?"

"Unless you see a donkey come by – or a UFO – that just happens to have extra space, honey, the answer to that is no. We have to keep truckin'." Mean Uncle.

As the sun continued its march, Robyn's resolve deteriorated and she announced her legs hurt. I made a rash decision: we would head for the Devil's Kitchen – Plan C – which would provide easier footing on a Jeep road toward home, albeit on a more roundabout route.

I cajoled: "You're doing great. Just a coupla more miles and we'll be on the home stretch." Sandbagging Uncle.

We were now in the Grabens, a series of parallel grass-floored valleys divided by vertical walls. Robyn announced she was sunburnt and miserable. Meltdown was imminent. We still had a ways to go. "Robyn, you've been magnificent. You are woman; hear you roar! Hang in there, and before you know it, we'll be drinking cold beer!" Compassionate Uncle. No: Sandbagging Uncle.

The Silver Stairs – rowdy Jeepers only need apply – were dispatched and we headed east for Elephant Hill, the going rolling and easy. We were golden and then … implosion. "Uncle Seany, I can't hike over Elephant Hill; it sounds too big! My legs hurt! I'm burnt! I love you and all that, but right now … I *hate* you!" Tears and anguish.

I didn't say a word. Bad Uncle. Horrible, Mean, Hate-able Uncle.

Robyn was hugged, then coaxed over Elephant Hill, a little bump really, and a ride was hitched back to our truck, Robyn making the transition from profoundly miserable to happy-go-lucky, laughing and dominating the conversation in the space of thirty-seven seconds.

In short order we were back in camp, the sun going down, relaxing in lawn chairs beside the fire in the comforting presence of distant cliffs glowing orange and purple. In no place else does time move so quickly or so slowly as in the desert, where the sky goes on forever, where ghosts speak in the sigh of the wind, where cliffs melt before your eyes. Robyn ate like a lumberjack, two heaping plates of spaghetti with garlic marinara, already talking about coming back again for the Joint Trail, a happy camper.

Mile of Truth

It was 2:00 in the afternoon by the time we convened at the base of the hill. We dropped our loads and caught our breath. Here, a trail coalesced and headed up the south side of the canyon.

This was the trail we'd used to access the canyon a few hours earlier, having negotiated a four-wheel-drive track along the rim for a few slippery miles. It was decided that Skylar and Nicky would retreat back up the canyon and bring down the rest of the bull while I shuttled loads up the hill to Skylar's truck, which we'd left tucked into a small opening in the trees near the edge of a large meadow.

Shouldering my pack, which held a hindquarter – it was heavy and required careful maneuvering – I made it a hundred yards up the steep trail before having to bend over and take a break. This was going to be, I accepted, more than I bargained for.

I'd received a phone call from Skylar the night before: "Sorry for calling so late. I've shot an elk. It's big. You wanna help me carry it out tomorrow? It's pretty remote." It was the "remote" that sealed the deal.

136

We left at eight in the morning, picking up Nicky down valley. In Naturita we got some gas station coffee and headed out for the Wild West End. Skylar had camped at Wildcat Reservoir before his hunt, hiking cross-country into upper Eagle Creek Canyon near the Utah border, where he'd made his kill.

Consulting an old topo map, we took a more direct line to the site, climbing up Ridge Road.

I'd been up this road earlier in the summer on a bicycle, during one of Henry Castigliani's famous pool party weekends, riding off a beer gut that had mysteriously appeared after a couple days lounging poolside. What had months earlier been a smooth bladed surface was now heavily runneled, the result, no doubt, of this year's heavy monsoons. If it got wet, this road would be snotty and not particularly safe.

Atop the ridge we continued on bumpy backroads to the spot where Skylar had hiked out of the canyon the evening before. Across the canyon, which looked at once wild, forbidding and inviting, lay another ridge, then Sinbad's Hole and Sewemup Mesa, the historical haunt of cattle rustlers and not too many others. Without delay we descended to the bottom of the canyon and proceeded upstream, the rivercourse with healthy flow, linking game trails along the banks. Presently we came to the cache, the carcass of the bull bigger than advertised, resembling a small mastodon actually, the meat in bags unmolested under a shelter of branches in the shade of a large boulder.

Although the day was sunny, snow was forecast and we didn't dally, cutting the legs at the knees, wrestling the loads into packs and retracing our steps. Back at the base of the hill we made our final plan and here I was now, bent over, gasping, contemplating the rim far above, one short mile, one small lifetime distant. I knew now – had known all along – that the next few hours would be spent deep inside the Reduction Chamber.

After a little mental self-flagellation, some self-mockery, a heavy dose of Zen and great physical exertion I was a hundred yards further up the trail and taking another mini-break. By the time I approached the rim with mud-caked boots and shaky knees, breathing heavily, the sun had fled many times, stars of the black night sky had wheeled in a blur, white dwarfs expanding, flaring and expiring, winter had come with deep drifts of purple snow and melted, tumescent buds had pushed from the branches of the trailside bushes, forest fires had raged down the side of the canyon, revealing slickrock bands of blood and bone, and I was done in. Forty-five minutes had past.

Then I had a brainstorm: I'd eat lunch. With half a peanut butter sandwich and a good slug of water coursing through my body I returned to the base of the hill and fairly bounded back up – ah, the miracle of food! – with a feather-light front quarter as burden. A bit of sleet on the cheek and a glance to the west announced the arrival of the promised storm, a solid gray wall now obscuring the upper canyon.

Back at the bottom our group reunited and we plodded back up the Mile of Truth a final time with a Honey Crisp apple our secret weapon, Nicky with the heaviest load giving a noble effort, truly Herculean. I was but a dumb beast, one foot in front of the other, knowing that the drive out of here was the real main event.

Skylar let his inner Monster Trucker out of his little cage and we emerged at Wildcat Reservoir in a snowstorm, bypassing the Ridge Road – not fancying cart-wheeling down the side of the valley and dying in a ball of flame – after a five-mile barely controlled fishtail, scrub oaks brushing both sides of the truck, back end swinging wide over yawning chasms, getting high-centered only once and able to retreat for a successful go. Night had fallen long since, tents of campers aglow with soft yellow light pulsating and comforting through the diagonal slash of the storm.

Lone Cone

In the past, it has been ignored in the pursuit of loftier peaks, yet been admired for its symmetry and regal bearing. As the years have passed and the warm temperatures of the canyons have lured us to the west and south, it has time and again reared up on the horizon, a pyramidal tooth, and presented itself as a unique and special mountain.

For eons, many more people lived on the tablelands and in the canyons of the Four Corners – indeed, at times more than live there today – than in the high mountain valleys we consider home, which were summer hunting grounds. It is easy to see that for these people the Lone Cone served as a beacon and magnet, an invitation, sitting as it does alone above the surrounding mesas, a universal point of reference.

It was in answer to an ancient call, then, that we finally decided to climb it on a recent Saturday morning. Driving to Norwood, we asked five different people there the best way to approach and climb the mountain and, almost predictably, received five different sets of directions. Deducing some common denominators from the different directions, we approached the mountain from the north, calves kicking in the fields, and presently found the desired trailhead. The Cone turned out to be one of the easiest mountains we ever drove up.

A short stroll up through some spruce delivered us to the Devil's Armchair, as the great north-facing basin of Lone Cone is called. It is this same boulder-strewn basin, purple in shadow, that had been regarded for the good part of one afternoon many Marches ago, from miles away to the north across Norwood Canyon, while sitting on a sun-warmed rock in an old abandoned roadbed at the top of Sanborn Park Hill. That day, the Cone had shimmered as a holy mountain while I sketched it, framed by the reaching fingers of the surrounding scrub oaks; I remember wondering if the raised hairs on the back of my neck were caused by a mountain lion attracted to the movement of my pencil on the page, or just by the brisk spring air.

Directly above us, the northeast ridge promised a short, quick and direct route to the top. A little exposed and involving some scrambling, it had been described as anything from an "easy Wetterhorn" to "you're gonna fall AND YOUR BONES ARE GONNA STICK OUT." Feeling lazy, we opted for the pedestrian northwest ridge, traversing the floor of the basin. Laziness will have its consequences, and it was here that we ran into trouble.

We had a casual time of it crossing the boulder field, and as we approached a grassy hillside that would bring us to the northwest ridge, I was remarking on the ease of our passage when my partner wobbled on top of a tipsy rock and fell slowly and awkwardly. Falling on her bum, she sat for a second, miffed, then extracted her hand from underneath her bottom.

The little finger on her right hand was bent 90 degrees sideways at the second knuckle. We inspected it closely and concluded it was dislocated rather than broken. At least there were no bones sticking out.

I announced I was going to grasp her finger and try to pull it back into place. Trying to be gentle and firm, I held her misshapen pinkie.

"OK, I've got it. Does that hurt?"

"No."

"OK, you ready?"

"Yes."

"You sure it doesn't hurt?"

"Yes, I'm sure."

"OK, I'm gonna pull it straight now. You ready?"

"Shut up and do it, would ya?"

With a slight tug the finger popped back into place. Relief. After sitting a minute to collect ourselves, we continued up the ridge and were soon on top. The views were even better than anticipated: the Sleeping Ute was right there, up close, as was the long dark ridge of Mesa Verde. Encircled by mountain groups, it was easy to see – and feel – that Lone Cone really is the center around which the local landscape and sky revolves, a gathering place for energy, a vortex.

To the north and west, a smattering of geometric shapes on a fertile green bench of the Uncompahgre Plateau, we realized, was Nucla. To the west, unfamiliar canyons and jumbled badlands beckoned and were put on the autumn touring schedule. I ate lunch too fast, felt a little reaction building and asked my partner to return the favor and pull my finger – this was cowboy country, after all, and when in Rome – but she cleverly declined. She's always been the mature one.

With clouds building, we retraced our steps down the ridge, across the basin, through the trees and drove happily across the dusty mesa, arriving home, as we rarely do, well before dark.

Sally W. Buffington

Sally Buffington is a writer of memoir, essays and poetry who lives in San Diego. She grew up in Massachusetts and views her life as bi-coastal. Educated at the New England Conservatory of Music and Mills College, for many years she was a flutist and private music teacher. Her literary areas of interest are nature and place, music, food and family. She is presently completing a memoir about her summer returns to Cape Cod.

AFOOT

The first steps were easy, across asphalt that I walked or ran over every day. So were the next steps over tire tracks of dusty, fine sand, pleasantly cool to the soles. It was only when I got to the top of the hillside and into the woods that my feet started complaining, whether I chose the gritty old blacktop drive (on which someone must have used up all the extra pebbles from miles around) or the pine-needled, pine-coned woodsy dirt. Prickly going, either way.

I walked a lot during my teen years, starting in 1957 when my parents bought Nauset Haven on Cape Cod, a summer 'cottage colony.' On part of our three acres of mostly wooded land, the cottages hugged the shore of a pretty spring-fed pond. To me it was haven indeed: a sandy beach for swimming, rowboats I could take off in any time I wanted -- and paths all over the place among the pines and oaks. Nauset Haven became my territory and I its primary citizen, free to explore just about every day, all year round.

Starting in mid June that first year and every summer after, I went through a private ritual of forcing my winter-tender soles to toughen up. No one said I had to. I just kept walking and walking until I could go anywhere without hesitation. Going barefoot meant that I felt fully in touch with the place: it was a point of honor.

With foot, and fingers, I stroked mossy cushions, pads of green velvet like islands spread among the pine needles. I scuttled along trails that led into thickets like private baskets to hide in. I tramped along the shore, happy to wear shoes when I encountered lots of pebbles. Oh, and empty mussel shells which, when they caught the sun, were shallow cups of pearliness. Some years, though, high water levels kept me farther back.

Standing on the edge of our little beach, I'd breathe in sun-warmed water, also an earthy summer smell mixed with blooming sweet pepperbush. Looking out over the swamp, I could pick out turtle snouts among the lily pads or lines of turtles sunning on a log. Water striders scribed the surface with quivery 'X's. Some winter days, I'd test a skim of ice with my toe and hear muted, confined cracks, a sound I imagined might occur as minerals split or sectioned within the earth.

Out in the late afternoon or early evening, mooey-sounding frogs serenaded me – no "ribbets" for this bass section. To this day, the calls of redwing blackbirds also take me back to the pond; so does any vista of a path in the woods.

As I walked, I talked to myself. Sometimes I sat down and read aloud parts from plays, hoping for an idea of who I was or might become. I was sorting things out. Though I didn't write in the woods, back in my room I kept a diary whose entries centered on making sense of life – parents, grades, friends, church, boys, and music lessons, all jumbled together in the pages.

Walking all over that lovely place in every season and recording my thoughts, I was learning to be myself.

When I go to Cape Cod now, those Nauset Haven years decades behind me, I stay in a large family cottage in another town. But I still have my summer rituals. I still take first steps.

The first day, weather permitting, I go to a nearby salt-water beach -- but making my way out to the waves is almost more interesting than swimming. First I trudge across a long expanse of soft sand, then a foot-testing strip six or eight feet wide of pebbles, wiry dried seaweed and shells: jingle shells, iridescent ivory or apricot in color, and slipper shells, dull gray white with pinkish or mauve lining. Yes, they're pretty! But jingle shells have sharp edges and coiled wiry seaweed's not very foot-forgiving, either, so I wince as I teeter across. Next I meet another strip, this one grainy, pebbly damp sand that gives a bit under my steps. Finally the water! Which by now feels especially cool and welcoming. Yet even as I shuffle contentedly over the soft sandy bottom, the occasional miniature crab nips my toe or heel.

Back from the beach, barefoot once more, I set out to further read where I am by circumnavigating the cottage. After crossing the front lawn, dodging twigs and pinecones among the grass, I turn and go down a gentle sloping path bordered by shocks of grass and weeds. The packed sandy-brown soil's partially covered by an assortment of pine needles, dry leaves, twigs, and tooth-sized pebbles, that Cape Cod ground so familiar from my pond years. My feet aren't as tough as they used to be, though, so I don't linger.

When I reach the back yard, the path turns to cement -- seventy-five year-old cement, that is. Pebbly and grainy, it's anything but smooth though my feet enjoy its coolness. Over the years sections have heaved themselves up so a plate here doesn't quite meet a surface there. The resultant tips and slopes make for dicey walking! I tilt to one side or the other, correct my balance and am reminded of walking aboard ship, as though our cottage were a big beached ark overlooking the salt marsh.

Oh, the marsh! Out there I walk with eyes only. Muddy, buggy ground, the marsh is home to herons, ospreys, ducks and crabs. Foxes and coons beat paths across; thousands of wood ticks dwell there, too. My husband and his brothers used to catch blue crabs and take day trips in a rowboat down the Centerville River that runs through. Officially declared a wetland by the state of Massachusetts, to me the marsh is sacred ground, wild, open land without people.

Then I turn and pad over scrappy grass by the clothesline and pass the kitchen steps; another turn and soon I'm back to the front yard. Now I carry out *tadasana,* the yoga pose known as "the mountain." First positioning the soles of my feet flat on the ground, I center myself and gradually align and position my entire body; finally I extend my arms upward. Complete. I've raised my focus from earth, from physical ground to the terrain of mind and heart, yet I encompass both, a metaphor for how I operate. Borrowing a term from Thoreau, I'm now fully "a sojourner in civilized life" -- and a barefoot self, even a naked one.

After walking, I often sit down to write – and look hard at my situation. Just as my body's matured from that of the barefoot teenager, I seek to go deeper looking at life now, to really know myself. At such times I might as well be naked.

As I was one humid August night, a few summers ago. Three a.m. Every bed in the cottage was occupied. Hardly a sound indoors or out. The leaves hung limp, the birds and usual humming insects enervated into silence.

Always my husband and I sleep in the buff and tonight I cannot imagine doing otherwise. Each of us lies in a flung position: he's zonked out but I'm wide awake. My mind rushes around on adult responsibilities. What to have for breakfast? Have we got enough eggs on hand? Who's leaving? Who arrives today? What on earth can I serve for dinner that everyone will like, and can eat? Telling myself to quit fussing, I turn to thinking how delicious the water felt this afternoon…oh, and my trail walk this morning, all that gorgeous fungus seemingly appliquéd on the tree trunks and the almost tropical density of leaves and vines and saplings…and I know I have to write.

Silently I get up, not bothering to put on a robe. I need no flashlight either as I start down the stairs to the living room. The stillness is thick and lovely, the air's almost furry on my skin.

"Sally?" A low voice.

Startled, I stop half way down and reflexively cross my arms in an X over my breasts.
Peering around, I make out one of our guests sitting on the porch in his pajamas, probably desperate for a smidge of breeze.

"Howard, are you OK? Do you need anything?"

"Oh, I'm all right. I just couldn't sleep and it's a bit cooler out here."

"Well, if you want a cold drink, help yourself to what's in the fridge. The light's on a string overhead as you walk into the kitchen." Then, hoping he's seen no more of me than legs and feet, I turn and scamper back upstairs.

I think back on that night now with only mild embarrassment – Howard probably thought, "Oh, here's someone else who can't sleep!" (Ever since then, however, I always put on a robe when I get up.) I envision myself as I must have looked, my naked figure white among

146

shadows and dark: a buxom ghost. And in that moment I see myself as the cottage's resident spirit, or perhaps Barrie's Peter Pan looking for his shadow when people are asleep.

My shadow? Whatever spiral-bound book I'm using for a journal this summer. I keep it on the desk, or if my guest-bedroom office is being slept in (as it was that night), in a corner of the living room. When I wake in the night, it's as though my journal waits for me in the dark, a rectangle whose luminescence only I can see. Picking it up, I switch on a light and sit down to write. Step one, a word or two, another, then a phrase, -- and my pen strides off over the ground of the paper.

Many times over the years, I've used the phrase "awake in the night" to begin such journal entries. Yet one of my favorite writing locations is very much a day place –the screened porch. I spread out papers and journal on the pull-up table, shuck my shoes, and lean back.

Take a breath.

Cardinals are whistling in the trees. Geese honk, church bells toll the hours. A squirrel vaults from a branch onto the rim of the birdbath, its tail a backlit question mark.

How the leaves shine in the light! Though if the wind's coming from the opposite direction, I see their backs instead, gray and suede-like. Surveying papery brown oak leaves on the ground, I virtually feel a dry crackle underfoot.

Sometimes I think back on an evening when we arrived at the cottage several summers ago. Those same trees bent and swayed and veered about in gusty winds, rustling and whooshing! I stood out in the dark and the wind whipped my clothes and blew them against my body as though I were a figurehead plowing through the seas. If I could have seen the wind, I think it might have looked like unruly giant airbags. Though buffeted and chilled, I felt welcomed. Cleansed.

Remembering and looking around, eventually I come to feel at the center of the dance of sounds and leaves and trees. As I write, they return to me the scattered parts of myself.

Even as I play my "awake in the night" role, though, I also write with others present, such as a day when friends were visiting. "Outside, glistening oak leaves and the sounds of large drops plopping from the gutter pipe. A *lovely* day to be indoors! Carl and Andy are playing Bach, and Pete's on the porch with the paper, coffee and radio for company. Kathy's holed up on the couch with a book. The house is a clutter of sheet music and newspapers, dropped clothes, books and magazines, Carl's oboe case, used coffee mugs – all accompanied by the watery percussion of rain." I looked out the window. "The screen's like a canvas -- no, it's an aqueous fabric with vertical lines of downward traveling water. Some drops stop midway, others descend like drops of translucent mercury. The newest and most prominent drips form slubs that look as though you could trace (yet not destroy) them with a fingertip. And through all this is visible a landscape of trees, branches bent low, and the white porch railing, a bright geometric structure pointed like the prow of a boat into the watery verdancy."

Restless, I thought, I've got to get out and explore! I grabbed my camera and pulled on a slicker, then went sloshing around admiring the uber-green of shiny wet leaves. So glistening were the oak leaves by side of the path, they looked like plastic. Soon my sneakers were soaked-- I might as well have gone barefoot in the first place. Looking out over the marsh, I found that the reeds, blurred by drizzle and mist, had taken on a wooly knitted look.

And as I walked, I realized, I'm the only one out here.

My favorite solo moments of all, though, still occur at night when everyone else is off in the little death of sleep. That's when the barefoot feeling translates to something beyond nakedness, an ability – always the desire, anyway -- to see myself and what I'm dealing with clearly. As though I could somehow x-ray myself by writing and my words would amount to footsteps, line after line.

Remembering that hot August night, I'm reminded of Duchamp's famous "Nude descending a staircase." I've always loved the shadowy overlapping states of the figure, the multiple exposure aspect of the painting. All at once, Duchamp conveys shifting states of mind, internal and external, as though his impressions were too much for one static image. Motion itself – walking -- is the most important reality. Finding a visual reminiscence of my naked summer experience, I see myself in the figure. A febrile, responsive soul full of ideas, I'm a moving "mountain" who walks and writes her way through life. The barefoot girl is still around, still searching.

Joey Lincoln

Hello, my name is Joey Lincoln, a native Vermonter, who moved to Denmark 30 years ago. I remain creative in my daily work, performing as a clothing constructor for Denmark's leading sports brand. I have three grown sons who have also learned the love of the out-of-doors but have never had the opportunity to experience a summer camp since they don't have them in Denmark. They have spent many summers in Vermont and love hiking, swimming and skiing, the most. I try to return home yearly, to stock up on peanut butter, pretzels and chocolate chip morsels!

SUMMER CAMP AT MEDOKAWANDA!

Summer vacations were always filled with wonderful camp experiences. Already at the young age of five years, I was sent to summer camp, to develop my social skills while participating in any outdoor activity offered. My first camp experiences were at local day camps, which, over the years, lead to weekly over-night camps and eventually, the best, out-of state camp, where I spent the entire eight weeks of my summer vacation, three years in a row, loving the activities, but most of all, the close relationships with people from all over the country. The friendships made there are everlasting.

When I say "the best summer camp ever," I'm referring to a camp in Washington, Maine, Camp Medokawanda. It was a BLAST! Medokawanda Camp was a girls' camp, where there was also a junior and senior brother camp, Medomak Camps. Thus, these three camps were run together, as one big happy family. All three camps were located on a beautiful lake, where many of the daily activities were

150

held. Even though the lake was about a mile hike through the woods from the girls' camp, we loved the walk to and from the lake. We would chat and laugh or even sing the whole way. Sometimes we were so hot, we would run the entire way through the woods to be the first to jump into the cool, refreshing water.

The days at camp were always packed –full of activities…there was never time to get bored. The activities offered ranged from every water sport imaginable to tennis, archery, arts and crafts, nature, theater, dance, and gymnastics. There were also two weekly trips out of camp each summer. The first trip was always a white-water canoe trip on the Allagash or another strong-current river, and the second trip was always climbing-up Mt. Katahdin, the highest mountain in Maine. Both trips were equally challenging, exciting and offered a perfect setting to really get to know the other campers and counselors. They were always the highlights of the summer and greatly anticipated.

The camps' biggest emphasis for activities was waterfront sports. They offered every imaginable sport done in water. My favorite was waterskiing. They had a mighty powerful speedboat that could pull five people at one time. We often entered contests against other local camps, competing on who could do the wildest tricks on one or two skis. Some were even so clever as to ski barefoot. It was great fun and it never really mattered if we won or not…it was just so fun to be a part of the competition.

The evenings at camp were also spent together, where planned activities were organized by the counselors, and they almost always ended with a huge campfire and lots of talking, singing and the weekly listening to one of the counselors reading a chapter of Winnie-the-Pooh. It was a magical time….all of us sitting in a circle around the campfire, staring at the flames, watching the sparks fly into the black sky, meditating on the day's wonderful activities and experiences, looking around at all the warm and happy faces around you…it was a beautiful way to end the evening. And if s'mores were served for good-night snacks….it made for very sweet dreams!

During the summer, all campers worked towards earning their "medals." To earn your medal, you must achieve three excellents, 10 high-honors and 16 honors by fulfilling different requirements in the assorted sports. After three summers of hard work, I finally earned my medal. The ceremony for this great accomplishment was to hold your own vigil. This meant deciding on a location for your all-night campfire and gathering enough firewood to last the entire night. We, of course, made sure there was a bucket of water handy, just in case, along with some warm clothes, a sleeping bag and a flashlight! I really don't remember eating anything but I'm sure the visitors probably came with sweet treats. We didn't have any small tents but if the weather report wasn't cooperative, we could make a shelter out of a tarp. Otherwise, if we slept, it was under the trees in the fresh evening air. We were just out in nature for the entire night, alone with our campfire. You were allowed to invite your three favorite counselors to visit you during the course of the night. Otherwise, you were alone with your campfire, staring into the flames, smelling the burning wood, listening to the crackling of the embers and the creaking of the trees around you. The woods was our "home" while at camp, so it was a relaxing, cozy and secure experience. OK, it could be a bit scary when you first heard noises in the distance. But shortly after you would see a flashlight and know that one of your invited guests was on her way. The counselor would sit for an hour or so and just talk to you, about you and camp and what it all meant to you personally. There were usually also a handful of compliments given from the counselor, which really warmed the soul and made the evening even more meaningful. It was an extremely special time, seldom felt in the hectic every day of camp life, with all the busy campers around. Before leaving, the counselor would hand you an envelope, which was filled with questions about life. When alone, there was plenty of time to reminisce on life and the things that are important. The questions were very philosophical, along with a tad personal, so they really made you think about life and God and what is really important to you in your life. You were asked to answer the questions and seal them in the envelope when done. This envelope would be collected by the next visiting counselor and saved for you until after the vigil was over.

The vigil probably started about 11:00 p.m. and lasted all night, where the counselors visited every other hour. It was your choice if you wanted to sleep between visits, or just enjoy the peace and beauty of the campfire. The sun would rise and the vigil would end. The camper would put out the remaining embers, pack up the campsite and return to camp for breakfast, with an experience nobody could begin to describe, if they never had tried it themselves.

At a special campfire ceremony, which included all three camps, the copper medal was awarded to the respective campers, in front of the entire camp and you were given your letters back. This was an honor and made you really feel proud of this personal accomplishment.

Camp Medokawanda had a huge influence on my life as a child and as an adult, and I wish every child in the world could have this same or similar opportunity to experience summer camp.

Barbara Miles

Basha (Barbara) Miles lives in an old converted carriage house behind a Victorian on the main street of Bristol, Vermont, where the Champlain Valley meets the Green Mountains. She delights in knowing that her writing space in the loft is most likely just above where the horse stalls used to be. She sometimes imagines that she can hear the horses quietly munching their hay or neighing in anticipation of being harnessed to a carriage. She and her dog enjoy daily walks in the village and the surrounding countryside. And, in addition to writing, she likes to read, draw, dance, meditate, garden, do tai-chi, and remember with fondness her conversations with deaf-blind children and their families.

GRAVITY, GRIEF AND GRATITUDE

What gets me out of doors regularly these days, where I live – here in a small Vermont village -- is my dog Bella, and her desire, need and enthusiasm for walking. Words almost sure to wake her, or get her to peer over the stair landing where she likes to rest, are, "Wanna go for a walk?! A walk, Miss Bella?" She learned those words pretty quickly, even as a very frightened dog that I adopted a couple of years ago. (Even frightened dogs love to walk, I discovered.) Since then I have been mostly following her around on our walks (no "heeling" for her, at least not yet) several times a day. These days Bella has been helping me discover what I imagine I would miss if her animal soul, her love of smells, her need for movement, and her curiosity, didn't remind me. Without her, I might be tempted to a life pretty much comprised only of sitting and reading and indoor comfort (or angst, whatever the particular day was like) especially since I am recently nearly retired from my professional life. Without Bella to draw me out of doors, it is possible (who knows?) that I could be living a couch-potato life. Which is kind of what I was raised to do.

I grew up in the suburbs of Washington, DC, where manicured lawns abutted manicured lawns, and where the adult pastimes were mostly confined to office buildings, living rooms, kitchens, and increasingly -- as I grew -- centered around the newly invented hearth of the black and white television. Television was such a novelty then that people (including my parents and my sister and I) often had a hard time tearing ourselves away. Even then, though, my child self had some of Bella's curiosity and wisdom – something that felt instinctual that pulled me out of doors away from the bewilderment that I often felt in the face of the television news and the seemingly constant talk of politics that my child mind couldn't make sense of.

One of my earliest specific memories of the out of doors was of being about 10 years old, being at home alone with my mother when she received a phone call telling her that her Polish mother, who was far away, had just been diagnosed with bone cancer. The news was shocking and upsetting to my mother, and she reacted by sending me outside to mow the lawn while she tried to make sense of what she had just learned (probably with the help of a cocktail or two). As a sensitive child, the only thing I knew for sure was that my mother was in great pain, and that there was nothing I could do for her. Nor was she in any position to soothe my own complete bewilderment and helplessness in the face of her tears. Going outdoors alone at such a time felt like a pivotal moment for me – without mother to lean on, on whom could I depend? What I discovered then was that I could depend on the ground itself, and on the trees, the wind in the leaves, even on the worms and ants crawling beneath my feet. I found that day, and many other times during my childhood, a life outside of my family's house that held and supported and watched over my family and myself in ways I am only just beginning to understand.

A few years ago I wrote a short story exploring through imagination the experience of that child, whom I called Monica. Here is what I imagined she might have experienced that particular day:

When she was done mowing, Monica took off her sneakers, tossed them toward the terrace, and walked barefoot on the newly-mown grass, pushing the mower toward the garage. When she came to the driveway and its smooth surface, just past the black walnut tree, she felt something awful under her toe. Yech!!! She screeched and recoiled at its gooshy texture, its ugly unfamiliarity. Her hands released the mower handle and she ran up onto the brick terrace. Safe (she presumed) from the worm. It was a long brown worm, a gooshy worm! Yuck!! From that distance she could no longer see it. It had disappeared from the tarred surface of the driveway, and must have gone into the soil beneath the grass. Monica sat down and held her big toe, the one that had stepped on the worm (the same one with blue crayon smudge on it). She rubbed the toe with her thumb, trying to erase the icky feeling.

Then she hugged her legs closely, and put her chin on her knees. She rocked back and forth, and squeezed her legs tighter. She felt very far from her mother, whom she still pictured on the tall stool in the corner of the kitchen, playing solitaire, drinking something cold, letting the radio drone on. Monica remembered the invisible Iron Curtain [between her and her mother], and nearly reached out to try to push it aside, but knew immediately that its invisibility made it un-pushable. Instead, she squeezed her knees with both hands, arms crossed.

Just then, an unexpected breeze kicked up, lifting the leaves of all the tall old trees in the yard, tossing their branches to and fro. Monica looked up, wondering if it was going to rain. No. It wasn't cloudy. Just breezy. The branches looked like they were old ladies' arms, flailing wildly, trying to get her attention. Monica imagined she saw a face in the middle of the tallest Kentucky Coffee tree. A big seed pod swooped up, looking like the wink of an eye above a gently curving branch. The branch reminded her of a smile she was somehow familiar with. Did her Grandma smile like that? Monica squinched her eyes shut and tried to remember how her Grandma smiled, or *if* she smiled. No luck. No memory of a grandmother smile.

Suddenly three black walnuts (whose outer shells were actually a kind of citrine green) fell, one after another – thud! thud! thud! – onto the freshly mown lawn. Monica opened her eyes. She unclasped her knees and stood. She went over to where one had landed, near the roots of the tallest of the trees. She picked up the walnut and put it to her nose, inhaling the odd, familiar, oily smell. When its odor reached her nose she became aware, too, of the just-mown grass smell, covering the lawn like a blanket.

Worms or no worms – it didn't matter. Monica lay down and buried her face in the soft short grass, clutching the walnut and holding it close to her face. She breathed in the kind-of-sad-smell of the just-cut lawn along with the oily black walnut smell. They smelled good together.

Her right eye, closest to the ground, was at just the right level to see an ant trying to find its way through the devastated forest of grass blades that lay all askew, asunder, in chaotic piles. The ant, Monica noticed, was really good at clutching the mown-down blades and making its way over the little piles. Monica liked watching the ant. She shifted her weight slightly so both eyes could track his progress.

After awhile, she became aware that the breeze had stopped. The only sound she could hear was her own breath. And a bit of rumbling that her right ear – now against the ground – was sensing. Something coming from deep down.

157

She found herself talking to the ant. "Pleeeze, little ant. Could you go to my Grandma and make her OK? Could you? Pleeze? She has cancer in her bones. I'm scared. Could you help her? Pleeze. Pleeeeeze. I don't want her to die, because my mommy is so sad. Roza is so sad. That's my mommy's name. Roza."

Her tears started to fall onto the grass blades, watering the devastated forest. The breeze started again, this time very, very gently. Monica heard it with her left ear. It was almost like a song. "Maybe that's my Grandma singing," was what Monica thought. "Maybe that's Magdalene." Monica knew that was her Grandma's name. She was pretty sure, anyway. Magdalene. That was her Grandma's first name. A Polish name. Her Grandma was Polish. Monica was sure of that.

"Sssszhchy, sssszhchy." That's what the breeze sounded like. It seemed like it might be a kind of Polish song that the breeze sang. That's what Monica thought, even though she had never ever ever heard a Polish song. It just sounded like it must be a Polish song. It had sounds that sounded like zzz's and shshsh's. Sounds like she remembered that her mother once told her that Polish had. Zzz's and shshsh's. Monica began to sing along with it. A little. Just a little. Not so anybody walking by would hear it. No. Just for the ant, that's all. The ant was the only, only, only one.

What I imagined as I wrote this story – imagined, I think, to have been true for me as a child because I know it to be true now as an adult – is that at a time of great bewilderment and uncertainty, even when the ground of certainty seems to have been entirely pulled out from under me, when things seem frightening and when there seems to be no human comfort to turn to – there is the ground, the comfort of roots and leaves and branches, the liveliness and playfulness of the wind, the persistence of even the smallest of creatures, and the holding power of earth itself, of gravity, and its bodily reassurance.

I remember a day fairly recently when I was at home here in Vermont working on my computer and I heard the news about the Newtown, Connecticut, shooting in which 26 children and adults at an elementary school died at the hands of a disturbed gunman. That news was utterly unfathomable to me, and so painful that it seemed like I could not bear it. I began to weep as the details of the scene emerged, and I began to wonder if I would ever be able to stop weeping. A mixture of grief, rage and utter bewilderment felt like a hurricane storming inside me, turning everything upside down. I remember a moment of looking up and seeing my dog Bella gazing at me. Seeing her gave me the impetus, even as I continued to cry, to rise and go out of the door with her. I put her in the car and we headed to the Watershed, a conservation area some five minutes away from my house in the village. All I wanted, all my soul wanted (and Bella reminded me that my own animal body wanted) was to be out of doors. And to walk. And walk. And walk. And walk.

Even by the time Bella and I got to the Watershed that day, I had already begun to feel some calm. The road there, almost as soon as it leaves the village, turns into a dirt road, runs past a big dairy farm, and then offers a stunning view of the Adirondack Mountains in the distance, across the expanse of the Champlain Valley. A vast view, which almost instantly puts a broad perspective on things. It is as though the mountains, just by their presence, announce not only a physical expanse, but also an expanse of time. As if they say with their blue-grey profiles, built from ancient granite, "Here we are, and here we have been, since before humans have walked this earth, and will likely be long after humans vanish." I might have remembered during that short drive to the Watershed, some lines of poetry that I carried in my wallet during the months after my own mother died some years ago, written by David Ignatow after his mother died:

Earth now is your mother, as you were mine, my earth,
my sustenance and my strength,
and now without you I turn to your mother
and seek from her that I may meet you again
in rock and stone. Whisper to the stone,
I love you. Whisper to the rock, I found you.
Whisper to the earth, Mother, I have found her,
and I am safe and always have been.

(David Ignatow, "Kaddish")

By the time I parked and let Bella out of the car, my tears had stopped, and we headed along the path leading up to the dam and the old reservoir. How was it (is it?) that walking on the earth -- under the branching pines and oaks, beside marshes, alongside the loamy forest undergrowth, past running water and still water -- so reliably calms the inner storms? I don't know, but I know it does. Perhaps it is something about the connection between my own rhythms and the great and small rhythms that surround me. (My childhood self seemed to know that, too, in some instinctive way.)

Bella stopped often, as she always does, to breathe in the smells. ("What in the world is she sniffing?" I often think, usually with an inner smile.) Her sniffing gives me pause and allows me to stop careening forward, which I am all too often likely to do, if only in my mind. When she sniffs I am given the opportunity to stop. Settle. Yield to gravity. Let the full weight of my body feel the soles of my feet. And wait for what appears. At these moments I often remember something a friend conveyed to me once as we were walking in the woods. He said that he had walked some years before with a Native American who had quietly mentioned as they walked in near silence that he makes it a practice to feel the curve of the whole earth with each footfall, aware of walking not only in the woods but on the great globe. I have not forgotten that, and think of it pretty often when I am walking with Bella or brought to stillness by her sniffing. These pauses – whether in the woods or on village sidewalks -- give me the opportunity to both feel the gravity of the globe that holds me and to see – really see -- whatever comes to meet my eyes in the moment.

That day I seemed to be greeted by rocks in particular, and most especially by a rock cairn near the edge of the expanse of reservoir. That cairn, with its carefully placed rocks and small offerings (many nearly invisible), spoke to me not only of what abides, before and after our brief lives as individuals, but also of those neighbors or strangers who had left little offerings or placed one of the stones. I imagined that they might have been people who, along with me, even though they were not present, were seeking a bit of what I was seeking, and finding it, maybe – a glimpse of a connection with the great mystery that surrounds us, with the stars from which the rocks (and we ourselves) came.

That day I happened to have a little pouch of turquoise beads in my pocket, one which I often carry when I walk, for moments like that one. Bella continued to sniff, and I took out a tiny bead, put my breath on it, held it in my palm for a moment, and found a little crack in the cairn where it looked like it would fit nicely. I may have spoken a few words. I'm not sure. Sometimes words come, and sometimes the silence is enough. I've left little beads (or cornmeal or tobacco) in many places as I walk, either alone or with Bella. It's an indigenous peoples' practice I learned some years ago, and it has gradually, over the years, strengthened my gratitude for all the mysteries I encounter out of doors (and sometimes indoors, too). It feels especially good to do this when I take something from the earth, when I pick flowers or vegetables, when I cut a branch, when I approach a place that seems especially beautiful or that touches me for one reason or another, or when an animal unexpectedly crosses my path, leaving me breathless, or when I come across a lifeless animal body that awakens my grief or bewilderment or praise for its life, or some combination of these emotions. At these moments, marking the spot with a concrete gesture seems fitting. That day, putting the tiny piece of turquoise into the cairn felt like a particularly small gesture in the face of what had happened, in the face of so much loss and bewilderment. But it was a gesture. One I could make. And did make, spontaneously, without even really thinking, just by following Bella into the out of doors.

And then I had the thought, as I stood there at the cairn, that soon the families and friends of those who lost their lives at Newtown would be making their own modern version of these ancient shrines – bringing their own offerings of flowers and teddy bears and photos and notes to some place, maybe the gate of the school building – to mark the place of tragedy. I was far away from Newtown, but for just a moment I felt connected in some natural and ancient way, with those people there.

Driving back to the village with Bella after our walk, I was aware that something had settled just a bit inside me. My sobs were over, and as we headed east it was the Green Mountains that appeared – the familiar curve of the particular cliffs that watch over the village. At least it seemed that way to me that day – that there was a presence always there, both above me and beneath my feet -watching, abiding, supporting -whenever I could remember to step out of doors and feel the curve of the globe underneath my feet and let myself see – really see – what is before me in the great outdoors.

Paul Fancher

Paul Fancher attended 16 schools by the time he graduated from high school. His dad was a doctor in the U.S. Army before, during, and after World War II and the Korean War. This essay/memoir is about fishing and catching things in the water while Paul was moving around and growing up.

He met Mary Kuhns in college at the University of Michigan. They married in 1954. They have four daughters, Katie, Janet, Lou, and Becky who all learned how to fish at an early age. Mary and Paul still live in the house they bought in Ann Arbor, MI in 1959. Paul is a Senior Research Scientist Emeritus at the U of M Transportation Research Institute.

YOU CAN'T CATCH A FISH WITHOUT A LINE IN THE WATER

This essay is about fishing and other natural phenomena associated with looking into the water. Fishing involves getting things done—packing up necessary equipment, getting bait, traveling to your fishing spot, putting a line in the water, and cleaning and cooking your catch. The fun is in the doing – in learning how to adapt to the adventures you face – in thinking about earlier experiences—in testing new ideas as you learn how to change challenges into opportunities.

Because my family moved around a lot, the scope of my boyhood adventures covers oceans, lakes, rivers, and streams. If a body of water is nearby, I want to move closer to see who or what is in it. Spotting something in the water is where this begins.

Challenges to Opportunities

I first got a line in the water in 1936 when I was four years old. We had recently arrived in Hawaii after a long ocean voyage from New York, through the Panama Canal to Honolulu. The U.S. Army paid for this trip on a luxury liner. They had assigned Dad to the medical clinic at Ft. Kamehameha, a small artillery base on the shore of Pearl Harbor.

Shortly after we arrived my parents gave me a toy boat. It had a propeller you wound up to make the boat go. The idea was to pick a rudder angle that would cause the boat to come back to you before the propeller unwound. Well, this hardly ever worked. So Dad would go wading out into the water to retrieve the boat. Although the water was shallow for a long distance I wasn't allowed to go off shore. This situation was frustrating for both Dad and me.

Dad tied a piece of fishing line to the boat. That way I could pull the boat in if it didn't come back. It was great fun for me. I liked it better than having the boat come back on its own. I started setting the rudder so the boat would go straight. Not only did I pull in the boat, I got to see how far it went. This was very exciting and I wanted to do it all the time.

There is more to this story. This was the peacetime Army, nothing like the wartime situation that occurred five years later. Our quarters on base came with a "striker", a young inexperienced recruit who spent part of each weekday doing what Mom asked him to do when Dad was at the clinic. Mom found our striker to be cooperative and reliable. She trusted him to take me down to the shore and send my boat out over the water. However neither of us were to go out farther than enough to launch the boat before returning to dry land. That was OK by both of us and we had fun doing it.

Late one afternoon when we were seeing how far the boat would go, we noticed something following the boat. When the boat got close enough we could see that the thing was an octopus swimming/crawling along the bottom just under the boat. I hesitated and, with the striker's encouragement, decided to pull the boat in steadily and slowly to see if the octopus would continue to follow it. It did. I got the boat close to shore and stopped pulling. The octopus stopped too. It remained sitting on the bottom next to the boat.

What were we going to do now? The octopus didn't move and neither did we. After some moments of this standoff the striker said, "Do not move and hold the boat steady." He went to get a rock. He returned, struggling with a heavy rock, while the octopus stayed right there, motionless. With great effort the striker thrust the rock at the octopus. As soon as the rock hit the water the octopus left with lightning quickness, leaving a dark spot behind.

As we were excitedly telling Mom about this Dad came home. Dad said, "Show me where this happened." When we got there, the octopus had not returned but the dark spot was still there. Dad said, "That dark spot is ink from the octopus." As far as I can figure out now, that's when I learned octopuses (octopi) produce ink.

This story serves as a metaphor for many new experiences I have been fortunate enough to have because I looked into the water hoping to see 'who–knows–what', (aka, 'whatever').

After I finished kindergarten, Dad got transferred to Tripler General Hospital in Honolulu. Our lifestyle changed. We moved from

Army quarters on the shore to renting a duplex apartment in Manoa Valley, a beautiful part of the city, well removed from any shoreline.

My parents loved the beauty of Oahu. Mom produced numerous paintings, etchings, wood carvings, and pottery serving-bowls in the shapes of tropical leaves while I was in the first and second grades at Punaho School.

Dad bought a hand–held Kodak 8 millimeter movie camera. He spliced together many small reels to make large reels. One large reel was entitled "A Trip around the Island." We made many trips around the Island of Oahu because the scenery was so beautiful and the distance around was about 25 miles and easily traveled in our car.

On one of our trips we saw whales jumping out of the Pacific Ocean. This was not planned. We made many trips around the island and this event only happened once. I am glad I was there because of how spectacular and dramatic it was and because my young eyes and brain could see and record those whales much more clearly than they appeared later in those old films.

Another large reel was entitled, " Flowers and Festivals." The number of planned festivals was huge and sometimes lasted longer than a little boy's attention span. However, near the end of our stay when I was seven years old and had finished the second grade, Dad took us to a Luau so he could film it and we could enjoy it.

Currently Luau means a Hawaiian party with traditional foods, Hula dancing, and other traditional entertainment. The Luau we went to had a special type of entertainment. It was held on a large beach. People were free to go in the ocean and many were wearing bathing suits. In addition to that, those of us in bathing suits got to help spread out a large net with floats on the corners. This was done early in the party and then we returned to shore to participate in the pageantry. Shortly before the food was ready to serve, we waded out into the ocean to help pull–in the net. I was amazed. The net was full of fish—many good sized fish. Anyone who wanted a fish for dinner got to pick their own fish, which was prepared wrapped in a leaf and roasted on the bed of coals used for roasting pork and other entrees. I ate very well that evening. Helping to catch the fish was great but eating what we caught made it even better.

We left Hawaii on an ocean liner in early September, 1939. We threw our leis into the ocean as the ship left Honolulu. The idea is if the tide takes your lei to the shore you will return someday.

Dad had time off for a long leave to see family and then was to report to the Mayo Clinic in Minnesota for a refresher course in medicine. This was standard practice for doctors returning from foreign service in the peacetime army.

When I was seven years old we returned to San Francisco. On the ship ride I enjoyed watching the flying fish as I had on the way over. This time Mom did not have to hold me down, fearing I would fall overboard. We landed in San Francisco on the day England declared war on Germany, a sign of things to come.

I could tell my parents were anxious to see their families. Mom and Dad had gone to high school together in Greensprings, a small town in northern Ohio, west of Cleveland. Dad had an older sister and Mom had a younger brother. Everyone knew everyone else in a small town like Greensprings. Mom's brother, Everett, had married and had a son, Gary, two years younger than I was. Dad's sister was an unmarried schoolteacher. I remembered her because she had visited us in Hawaii and gone on the trip around the island in which we saw the whales jumping.

Mom seemed to me to be concerned about England declaring war. Perhaps this was because she told Dad about her concerns when we were living Hawaii. People in a small town pay attention to neighbors and evaluate what they hear. They question unusual activities. "They have no good reason to want to know that" is an expression Mom used.

Mom was already suspicious of the Japanese and was concerned about their activities. By an old treaty Japan owned the fishing rights around Oahu. This meant there were Japanese fishing boats, sampans, in Pearl Harbor most of the time. Every so often one of those boats would be caught with a radio transmitting the location and type of every naval vessel in the Harbor. The radio would be confiscated and the owner of the sampan punished. The local Army and Navy authorities did not consider this an imminent threat. Mom's reaction was different and she felt strongly "they had no good reason to want to know that." She felt the situation needed attention before something bad happened. She was right to be concerned and our lives on the mainland changed drastically after the Japanese bombed Pearl Harbor in 1941.

Nevertheless I learned a lot about fishing before Dad went overseas during WWII. When Dad completed his refresher course at Mayo Clinic he was assigned to Ft. Hayes in downtown Columbus, Ohio, as the second in command of the medical facility. We moved into huge old quarters with high ceilings and windows to match. Although the world situation looked bleak this was still the peacetime army. This gave me the opportunity to learn about the type of fishing my parents had done as they were growing up in Ohio

I recall half-day fishing trips to spots along the Scioto River. Dad would hear of good places to fish from his colleagues and we would pack up our fishing gear, get some bait (usually worms – night crawlers), and head for the river. I don't remember any special fish but we usually caught enough bullheads, catfish and sunfish for a meal.

I learned how to handle a cane pole, keep my line out of the bushes and trees, bait my hook, and not fall in the river. I concentrated on my bobber so hard I could still see it in my mind when I closed my eyes to go to sleep the night after a fishing trip.

There was one special event I remember well. Dad was driving across farmland toward the river. We were following two sets of wheel tracks with grass in the middle and fields on either side. For a fee the farmer let us use this path to go fishing. I was in the front seat with Dad and Mom was in the back. We were bouncing around in the car as we progressed slowly toward the river. Suddenly Mom said, "Stop the car." Dad stopped abruptly, Mom got out, walked back about 30 feet and picked up something from the side of the path. She had spotted a four-leaf clover and brought it back to show us. Dad looked at it in disbelief. I don't think he had ever found a four-leaf clover even when he looked for them. He knew Mom had found them before but to spot one from a moving car was too much for him.

As for me, although I have never spotted one from a moving car, I have found many and continue to do so, thanks to Mom's inspiration and guidance. I am not sure how it works, but my eyes have learned the pattern of the clover. I tell people, "You don't know what a four-leaf clover looks like" or "You are wasting your time looking at three-leaf clovers. Shift your gaze from them immediately and find a four-leaf one to look at." None of this advice seems to help those who have never found one, and those who have don't need it. Apparently it is one of those things in nature you discover by trying to do it until your eyes get it.

One summer, I think it was between third and fourth grades, we went on a week long fishing trip to a cabin on East Harbor on Lake Erie. Dad, Mom and Everett had gone to East Harbor when they were in high school. They knew the fishing in East Harbor was good and if the white bass were running in schools you could catch a lot of them from the shore near Sandusky Bay Bridge.

We had invited Horace, son of the commanding officer, to go with us on the trip. He was a year older than I, but his experience on vacations had been to resorts with elegant accommodations, not to a basic cabin with a rowboat. My Uncle Everett, Aunt Alice, and cousin Gary came over from nearby Toledo several times during our stay.

As soon as we got unpacked Horace, Gary and I took our cane poles out on the dock to catch some fish. Horace had never fished with a cane pole. When a fish would bite he took a step backwards to help lift the pole and pull the fish in. But his step back took him off the dock and into the water. Mom gave him another set of clothes to wear, put the wet ones on a line to dry, and sent him out to fish again. It wasn't long before Horace repeated the step, fall, get wet maneuver. Mom gave him another set of clothes, observing that he had brought three sets of clothes in addition to those he was wearing. When Horace stepped off the dock for the third time Mom said, "If you do that again I am going to start over by giving you the first set of wet clothes." It worked out because Gary and I convinced Horace to sit down on the dock before he put his line in the water, and he didn't fall in again.

Later in the week the three of us went out in the rowboat. We had life jackets on. Horace and I each had an oar while Gary sat in the back of the boat telling us which way to go. Horace and I could not stay synchronized and tended to spin the boat around rather than make much forward progress. After a time we had moved to the center of East Harbor and were drifting toward the outlet into Lake Erie.

Uncle Everett had been watching and decided to row out to us. I was happy because I thought he would help pull us in. Gary had been saying that we didn't know how to row and I believed him.

When Uncle Everett reached us he said, "Come back in. You are getting too close to Lake Erie." Then he rowed off a little way and watched us struggle to make progress toward the dock. There was no offer to tow us in, but he did give us some pointers on rowing. First he told us to stroke together even if it meant going slowly. Horace and I were to cooperate and not compete. We managed to travel in a straight line but progress was slow. Uncle Everett suggested we take turns rowing. Our arms were just long enough to hold both oars at the same time. We could do it and as long as we were careful to pull equally on each oar we could make some progress as the other guy got to rest. We were worn out when we reached shore but we had learned about rowing.

The following year when my uncle was helping me learn to ride a bike I understood he wasn't going to do it for me, and I learned quickly.

There was another lesson about fishing on the trip to East Harbor. Towards the end of the week, Gary, Horace and I had become good at catching fish off the dock. Some of the older folks didn't do as well in their boats. One day a large school of rock bass came in around the dock, unseen by others until we three started hauling in fish and whooping it up. Dad and Uncle Everett came to see what was happening, followed by people from other cabins. That was the end for us. We were asked/told to get off the dock so that others could enjoy the fishing. We thought that we had found the fish and they were ours to catch, but that's not how it works. In their desire to catch fish, other fishermen will take over the territory. It is no wonder fishermen tend to keep their places and methods secret.

On the other hand, every cabin had plenty of fish to eat that night. Later we were treated as heroes. Maybe it is not so bad to share your good fortune once in a while.

At the time of the Pearl Harbor attack Dad was in command of the medical facilities at Ft. Hayes but my residences changed quickly after that. According to notes Mom kept we lived in the following places:

Chester, VA from 1/42 –6/42

Farmville, VA from 6/42–10/42

Medford, OR from 10/42 –12/42

Portland, OR from 12/42– 2/43

These changes entailed a lot of packing up, shipping furniture, driving across country and finding places to live. Dad was assembling a general hospital unit to go overseas to treat the sick and wounded. The moves were required to get his unit organized and trained for operating in the field. (Although none of us knew what would happen later, the unit became the 76th General Hospital. After the Normandy invasion Dad's unit moved from England and set up with 1000 beds in tents on high ground overlooking Liege, Belgium.) Besides getting his unit ready, Dad had slipped a disc in his back while moving a foot locker and had ended up in the hospital with his legs paralyzed. After an operation he recovered enough to be allowed to remain in command of his unit.

During this time period I finished the second half of fifth grade in Chester, VA. On my way to school I followed a small brook about two feet wide and about six inches deep. The terrain was somewhat swampy and the flow of water was steady all year round. One day on the way home, I was looking in the water as I usually did, and saw a small turtle, black with yellow markings. It was the size of the palm of my hand and I picked it up and carried it home. The turtle pulled its legs, head and tail into its shell and kept them there until we got home.

At home our landlord provided an old style metal washtub for the turtle. Now that I knew there were turtles to be caught I was on the lookout for more. Soon I had 13 turtles in the tub. The day after putting the 13th in the tub I looked and counted only eight. What happened? Had they managed to crawl out?

I told Mom about this and asked how it could have happened. She said, "A little boy knocked on the door and asked if he could please have a turtle." She said she had been wondering what to do with all of them, and this seemed like a good idea. "So I gave him one. A little later some other children came and asked for turtles." After some negotiations with Mom I was able to keep one or two for myself, while she could give away any extras.

This meant I could still look for turtles but didn't need to bring them home. One afternoon when I was checking out the turtles I saw something I had never seen before. Looking closely I could see it was a big turtle. Its shell was about a foot long and eight to ten inches wide. There were no yellow marks. When I poked it with a stick it didn't pull its head into its shell. I could see there would be a problem picking up the turtle but I wanted to take it home. I wanted to show it off to Mom, Dad, and our landlord. I liked the landlord –we would talk together and play catch. He was a sports editor for the main paper in Richmond, VA.

Well, I took the turtle by the tail. Its tail was long enough that I could pick it up in a way that avoided being scratched by its hind feet. I held the turtle at arms' length to avoid being snapped by its mouth or scratched by its front feet. Although the turtle seemed lighter than I expected, I wasn't sure I could carry it home without having to put it down along the way. As I walked along my arm got tired. Luckily I spotted a low hanging tree limb where I could rest my arm and not have to let go of the turtle's tail. In the process I figured out how to use my left arm to help carry the turtle. First I extended my right arm with the turtle out in front of me. Then I supported my forearm with my left hand, with my left elbow digging into my stomach and helping to carry the load. With this arrangement I made it home and deposited the turtle in the washtub.

The landlord arrived home from work before Dad. He was looking at the turtle when Dad arrived. He already had plans for the turtle. He told Dad he had an old family recipe for turtle soup and Dad was intrigued. Our landlord was a native of the region and knew who to contact and what to do to make turtle soup.

The first thing we did was to take the turtle over to the 'Court House' —a neighboring small town and the county seat. The local expert in cutting off turtle heads lived there. He enticed the turtle to snap on a stick and lock its jaws. That way the turtle would not let go of the stick and the executioner could use the stick to extend the turtle's neck while he chopped the turtle's head off with one stroke of his hatchet.

After that the assembled crowd discussed how to clean the turtle to get the pound of flesh needed for the soup. It became apparent after awhile that none of the locals were going to do more than give advice. Although Dad had never cleaned a turtle he had cleaned and dressed animals before, so he said he would work on the turtle.

When we got home we ate dinner and then Dad and I went to work on the turtle. We encountered many obstacles. The skin was really tough and our knives had trouble penetrating it. The back shell and bottom plate were hard to get apart. The legs had about 1/2 pound of meat on them. The other main muscles were high in the shell, attached to bones which formed braces across the middle of the shell. After a great deal of time and effort Dad was able to get some more meat and declared it enough to make turtle soup. And then he announced, "I will never operate on a turtle again."

Our landlord had been out that evening gathering other ingredients for the soup. This entailed talking to old-timers to learn of special items to add to his family recipe. By the time he finished we had enough ingredients for a big pot of soup, with or without the turtle meat. All of us enjoyed the meal and the adventure stories we had to tell. It was a fitting celebration to mark an extraordinary set of events. I hadn't imagined what bringing home the turtle would mean.

The next stop in our travels was Farmville, VA. Mom and I lived there alone. Dad had slipped a disk in his back. He was either in the hospital getting his back repaired or, when well, working full time organizing the unit he commanded. I remember riding my bike a lot when we were in Farmville and Mom saying we were going to stay near Dad because he needed us.

When we got to Medford, Oregon, I was amazed by the huge fish I saw in the Rogue River. Even though the current was fast the fish crowded into pools and did not move. I wanted to try to catch one but was told these were salmon that had spawned and now were dying and decaying. They were no longer fit to eat.

I was in school for less than a month when Dad's outfit was moved to Vancouver Barracks on the north side of the Columbia River in Washington State. We lived in a lumber baron's mansion in Kings Heights, overlooking the city of Portland, OR. This huge house had been divided into several apartments to meet the demand for housing. Workers for Henry Kaiser's factory for building Liberty Ships used in transporting goods overseas had doubled the population of Portland. The whole city had to adapt. There were twice as many kids and to accommodate the schools operated two shifts, morning and afternoon. The same teachers taught both shifts.

By state law students in the 6th grade had to study Oregon history. Most of the history was about the Indian tribes and the early settlers. I learned that the Indians were given special fishing rights in the Columbia and Willamette Rivers. They were allowed to net salmon using long poles on a mechanism for lifting fish from the river. This mechanism would then rotate or swivel to unload the fish.

I didn't get to go fishing but Dad did. He caught Silverside salmon in the Willamette River, close to where it joins the Columbia. He went out with a boat operator who took people fishing for a fee. On Dad's first trip he caught an eight-pound Silverside and we had lots of salmon steaks. Then he came home with another silverside about a pound heavier. Good thing we all liked eating fish. The third time was different. As I remember the story Dad caught a small silverside on this trip but the boat owner offered him a deal. He, the owner, would keep Dad's fish for himself and in return would give Dad a 20-pound Chinook salmon he had caught earlier in the day. Well, Dad came home with the Chinook and hung it up on the balcony of our third floor apartment. This balcony overlooked the front entrance, which had giant (fake) pillars holding up the front roof which extended over the balcony. The fish was up there for a couple of days in cool weather until Dad got it cleaned, cut up and distributed. Those living in the apartments got some, Dad's fishing buddies got some and we still had plenty.

For training purposes, Dad's outfit went on bivouac and set up as a field unit. I got to go along for part of the time. One of the doctors, Major Justice, took me fishing in a trout stream. He had learned to fish and hunt in the hills of North Carolina. I had a lot to learn about trout fishing and wading in a stream. In the past I fished from the bank or from a boat. I had already learned to avoid getting my line tangled in trees or bushes but I needed to learn how to avoid scaring the fish when walking downstream or upstream. I had to learn how to spot likely locations for trout, whether trout were feeding on insects in a pool, and how to get to a spot from which I could make a good cast. I managed to catch a few trout, nothing big, but enough to give me a feel for hooking and netting a fish. It was a great experience. It helped me "think like a fish" as Dad would say.

In February of 1943 Dad's unit left in secret. Mom and I knew the day they were to depart on a train but that was all. Dr. Perry, the unit's eye surgeon, and Dad had gone to medical school together in Ohio. They had arranged for Mom and me to stay with Mrs. Perry and her daughters until we found an apartment in Upper Arlington, Ohio, a suburb of Columbus. When Dad was at Ft. Hayes we were able to live off base in Upper Arlington for a year when I was in fourth grade. The apartment we found then was about three blocks from the one we moved into during the war. This meant we were familiar with the school and Mom and I knew many of the families.

The trip to Upper Arlington from Portland was tough. Fortunately the wife of a young doctor in Dad's unit needed a ride to Iowa. She helped drive to Davenport, Iowa. Mom drove the rest of the way with me and our dog "Ding" that we had inherited from another army family. When we left Portland it started to snow. We had chains put on to help get over the mountains in eastern Oregon. Along the way, on a dry section of road, the chains caused a flat tire. We got help changing the tire and limped into Pocatello, Idaho, to get a new tire. This was wartime. The national speed limit was 35 mph or less all the way across the country. In addition tires were rationed. When Mom pulled into the car repair shop the owner told her he could not sell her a tire until the ration board met and approved the sale. The next board meeting would be the following week.

Mom explained our situation. Their husbands had left Portland for an unknown military destination, they were two women with a little boy and a dog traveling to the Midwest to stay with family until the war was over. The owner took pity. He happened to be on the ration board and he took off to talk to the other members. Somehow they decided he could sell a good used tire to us with their approval. He sent us on our way without chains because the wind would blow the snow off the road in Wyoming. He was right about that.

The rest of the drive was long and tedious. I remember one night in particular. We stopped driving after dinner at a motel in Ogalala, Nebraska. It was seven degrees below zero. Nevertheless Ding and I played in the snow until Mom made us come in. She said we needed our rest for the next long day cooped up in the car.

With Dad away and Mom worried, there weren't any fishing trips until he came home in 1946. The war's challenges delayed us but its end brought new opportunities to go fishing together again.

After helping set up hospitals for the army of occupation in Europe Dad was assigned to Washington, D.C., to participate in assembling a medical history of the U.S. Army during WWII. This job had regular hours and free evenings and weekends, and time to go on leave. We headed for Chesapeake Bay to catch fish and/or crabs on several occasions.

One afternoon Mom, Dad and I were fishing from an abandoned pier. The tide was coming in and the deck was about ten feet above the water level. We were using shrimp for bait. We would cast out as far as we could and let the line sit, "still" fishing, waiting for a bite. Mom was good at this. She sat down on the deck with her legs out in front of her. When a fish bit Mom rolled onto her back to set the hook, then came back up to reel the fish in.

We caught several nice fish. "Nice fish" is a description frequently used by sport fishermen. These particular fish were called "croakers" because of the sound they made after being out of the water for a while. We had our fish in a wet burlap bag to keep them from drying out in the sun.

A man walked out on the pier and told us the fishing was not good off the pier. He suggested other places to go to catch fish and rent a boat. Mom, Dad and I looked at each other without saying anything. All of us were hoping the croakers didn't croak. We were afraid the man would join us if they did. We told him we were just happy to get our lines in the water. Then he said goodbye and wished us luck. We thanked him and nodded a thanks to each other as he walked away.

On another occasion we rented a cabin on a small bay off the Chesapeake for a weekend. The cabin had a dock, which we used for crabbing. Our version of crabbing worked this way:

1st, you tied a fish head to about 20 feet of heavy string.

2nd, you tossed the head out into the water and let it sink.

3rd, a crab started dragging the fish head away while eating the flesh

4th, you pulled the crab slowly so it would continue to eat and not let go.

5th, once the crab got close you slipped a long handled net under it and lifted it out of the water.

Of course this describes the ideal situation. At that time Chesapeake Bay was full of crabs so that steps 1, 2, and 3 were not a problem. However steps 4 and 5 required finesse. You were lucky if you caught seven or eight out of ten crabs that took the bait.

On one particular day we were doing well, taking turns in pairs with one person pulling in the crab and another netting it. We had invited another family to visit us at the cabin to help catch crabs and then feast on our catch. Their son John was a quick learner and good partner for me. We caught our share of crabs and put them in a large cardboard box holding all the other crabs.

When it was time to boil the crabs my partner wanted to carry the box up to the cabin. Since John was a guest that was fine. He was short and plump around the middle and wasn't wearing a shirt. He was doing well holding the box against his stomach and we were about halfway back to the cabin when one of the crabs found a small opening. It pinched John's stomach, he threw the box into the air, and when the box landed on its side all the crabs scrambled out and headed for the water. It is said that crabs know instinctively the way to the water and these did. Those of us with nets began catching the crabs in the grass and putting them back in the box. We managed to get nearly all of them. This time John held the box away from his middle and delivered the crabs to Mom who dumped them into boiling water.

A crab feast is great if you like the meat, but even if you don't, catching crabs for a party is great fun. Just don't get pinched by a live one.

A more serious warning has to do with casting. I learned this the hard way. We were at Chesapeake Bay with army friends. Their son, Joe, was a year ahead of me in school. Later in life we both became engineers but at this age he was already absorbed in designing and building new things. I was more interested in football, basketball and baseball as extracurricular activities.

While our parents were talking Joe and I went out on the dock with our casting rods. We didn't go there to fish. We had tied six-ounce sinkers to the ends of our lines and we were seeing how far we could cast. Whether you think of it as an engineer or an athlete you find out the length of your cast depends upon the speed of the weight at the moment you take your thumb off the reel and let the line unwind freely.

As it turned out, most of my casts went farther than Joe's, but when his timing was good his casts went about the same distance as mine. We started taking turns, making the exercise into an unintended competition. We were both right-handed and Joe was to the right of me. He would cast first and then I would try to out distance him. This all ended when Joe started a cast, realized his timing was poor and did not take his thumb off the reel. Instead of going out into the bay the sinker swung around at great speed and struck me on the left side of my head. I remember trying to keep standing and not black out. When I came to, Dad was kneeling beside me and asking me to talk to him. Although I felt okay except for a sore spot on my head I was not allowed to do anything but sit for the rest of the day. Joe felt much worse than I did. He had been scared and could not get the picture of my fall out of his mind.

In hindsight I realized I had been told to not go near anyone swinging a bat or golf club, but no one told me to stay away from a person casting a fishing line. This can be tricky when two or three people are fishing from a small boat, but in general, everyone needs to watch out for the others. There is a joint responsibility.

After a few months Dad was sent to Washington University in St. Louis to take an advanced medicine course. He was preparing for an exam to be board certified in internal medicine. The army wanted their doctors to become specialists or administrators. Dad's promotion to higher ranks as a medical doctor depended upon being board certified.

There wasn't time for fishing in St. Louis. However, on the way there Dad stopped to see an old friend in Waldo, Ohio, between Delaware and Columbus on the Olentangy River. The friend was a doctor who had recently retired from the army and returned to private practice. The two had lots to talk about so I brought along my rod and reel and a couple of lures to go fishing while they talked.

They let me off at a convenient spot with easy access to the river. I was to meet them two hours later at the same spot. The lure I chose looked primitive even in 1946. The yellow body looked as if someone had sawed off about 3 1/2 inches of a wooden broom handle. The cut was at a 45-degree angle. The slanted surface was painted red. You tied the line to an eye–screw near the upper back of the slanted front, that way the lure would dive and waffle side to side as it was reeled in. Underneath it had two sets of treble hooks, one at the middle and the other near the rounded end. I could tell that when the two doctors saw my lure they didn't expect me to catch anything but they kept quiet.

When I got down to the water I saw a man in waders walking up stream and casting into the deeper pools where the water slowed down. I waited for him to move on, then followed a good distance behind. I tried a few casts along the way but mostly I was watching how he fished. It reminded me of trout fishing but he was using a casting rod, not a fly rod. When he reached a bigger pool he stopped walking and made many casts into it. Once, when reeling in he jerked the rod but failed to hook the fish. He cast several more times before moving on.

I decided to try my luck and cast into the pool. I did not have wading boots but stood in water up to the tops of my sneakers. On my third or fourth cast I hooked a nice bass. The fisherman ahead saw me struggling to bring in the fish without tangling my line in weeds or broken branches. He came back to the other side of the pool to watch. When I worked the fish into shallow water I realized I had no net and didn't know what to do. I yelled to the man, "What do I do now?"

"Beach the fish." And that's what I did. I followed a sand bar to the shore and dragged fish into the grass along the bank. I found a stick, shoved it through the gills and out the fish's mouth. Now I could keep the fish under control. By that time the fisherman had come over to see if I needed more help. He looked at the fish and the stick and smiled. Then he looked at my lure in amazement. He had a hard time believing what he had seen but there was no doubt my lure had caught the fish. I told him I was fishing while my dad was visiting in Waldo and I was going to take my fish and go back to my pickup spot. He congratulated me and gave me a good-sized sunfish from his creel. I thanked him for the fish and for telling me what to do with the bass, saying I would have lost the fish without his directions.

When Dad and his friend came back I was sitting waiting for them, wanting to be on time and surprise them with my fish. (I went all through college and the years before it without wearing a watch. I didn't like rings or bracelets or watches on me. I used to have a sense of time, which I lost by staying inside and looking at my watch in later years.)

Dad and his friend were dumbfounded by my catch. They studied the lure and tried to explain how it attracted fish. With my boyhood logic I knew it attracted fish because I cast it in front of a hungry fish. What difference does it make after the fact? I had learned to go with what you got and do the best you can.

Next stop after Dad passed his board exams was in Battle Creek, MI. We lived in a house on the Kalamazoo River, in the country about ten miles from town. In the spring I found I could catch large carp in the river. The river's banks were lined with trees, bushes, and undergrowth. Careful manipulation of a long cane pole was needed to lift the carp out of the water and into an open spot where I could grab it. The first carp I caught weighed about five pounds. I had never caught a fish this big before and took it to show Mom. She was impressed and since it was cool outside with no bugs, we spread in on the grass where Dad would see it on his way in. He looked at it and wanted to know how I caught it.

After I told him, they changed the conversation. They both knew I wanted to eat the carp for dinner but people they knew did not eat carp. Carp are said to have a strong taste resembling the flavor of mud. Nevertheless Mom tried baking a big hunk of tail meat in the oven. It tasted like mud, and smelled bad too.

Mom, knowing some people do eat carp, decided to investigate the possibilities. We tried a number of approaches. We cut out what is called the "mud vein". That didn't help. After a couple more experiments we decided people didn't eat carp from the Kalamazoo River and we used them to fertilize the garden. We raised wonderful vegetables that year and Dad revived a worn out strawberry patch. He dug up the older plants, replacing them with carp parts for fertilizer. The carp were not good to eat but they contributed to good eating.

After a year of living in the country we moved into Battle Creek. Dad was made Chief of Medicine at Percy Jones Army Hospital.

Before the war the building had been part of the Kellogg Sanitarium, which meant it did not look like an Army hospital. It had a magnificent lobby with rugs and easy chairs, big couches and pillars up to a high ceiling. When we lived in the country I would walk over to Percy Jones from school and wait in the lobby for Dad to finish work. I would sit in one of the chairs and take a nap. Dad could identify with this since we both were known for being able to nap anywhere, anytime. However he did not want his colleagues to see him waking his son from what appeared to be much needed rest.

For me the move to town had big advantages. I had grown from 5'4" to 6' during ninth and tenth grades and gone from being a possibility to being a good candidate for the football, basketball and baseball teams in the 11th grade. Although fishing was important, as far as I was concerned there were three seasons –football, basketball, and baseball.

The move had advantages for Dad too. He had more latitude in arranging his schedule. In his position he had reason to check out the rehabilitation facilities for patients who were severely wounded or who had developed mental illnesses in WWII. These facilities were west of Battle Creek at Ft. Custer, where Dad discovered three lakes. Eagle Lake was close to the rehab facilities housed in refurbished army barracks. Mobile patients could go down to the beach and fish as a means of raising their spirits. Hart Lake was larger than Eagle and closer to town and used mainly as a fishing area by military personnel. The third, smaller lake was formed naturally by a rocky area blocking the flow of a small stream. We fished in all three lakes.

Dad's colleagues tended to fish at Hart Lake for bass and bluegills, good fishing when they were biting. However Eagle Lake became our favorite. One afternoon when I came home from football practice Dad was already home, waiting for me on the front steps. Next to him were two long, thin fish, about two pounds each, looking like nothing I'd seen before. Dad said he caught them at Eagle Lake and said they were Northern Pike. He had taken one of the rowboats on the beach and rowed out into the lake before casting, using a spoon lure with red and white paint on top and shiny silver on the bottom. I was ready to try my luck on Eagle Lake.

Fishing for pike from a rowboat provided new challenges for me. I was slow at getting my leaders, snaps and swivels ready to attach my lure. In addition it took different timing to cast with the lure at the end of a long leader. At first I often got backlashes when I didn't use my thumb properly to modulate the rate the reel was spinning. Also I often hesitated before casting because I didn't want to hook Dad in the back swing, I didn't want to cast across his line, and I was trying to figure out where the fish were.

I should have mentioned that Dad looked at challenges and saw opportunities. In this case he said, "You can't catch a fish without a line in the water." Well, first of all, that's an obvious statement, and second, I was obviously having trouble getting my line in the water, and third, I had heard this kind of statement from Dad before. ("You can't get a hit unless you go to bat.") I knew he was telling me I was capable of learning to cast properly and I would catch fish after I did.

When the baseball line was delivered I had been looking for sympathy. It made me realize that if I wanted to be a ball player I needed to get hits. I went up to bat trying to get a hit after that. Dad didn't need to repeat that message. However fishing was a different deal. It took a few fishing trips for me to get things sorted out and organized. Dad had numerous opportunities to say, "You can't catch a fish without a line in the water." Those words were said with a smile, and I smiled back unless I had a particularly difficult backlash to untangle.

After several trips to Eagle Lake Dad and I realized we took up time casting without finding where the fish were. We started trolling with our lures far behind the boat as one of us rowed slowly around the lake. It took about an hour to row completely around and more often than not we caught a pike big enough to provide dinner for all three of us. We found several places where we were more likely to catch a pike. These spots were scattered uniformly in a way that it made sense to row around the lake.

Although Dad and I had many successful fishing trips at Eagle Lake we never caught a really big fish, but others did. I saw three of these cases and heard of a fourth. The fourth involved a fellow recovering from mental illness. His treatment at the hospital had been successful and he was sent to the rehab center at the lake. He was allowed to go fishing as part of preparation to return to civilian life. He hooked a 20-pound Northern Pike and after a lengthy struggle managed to get it in the boat. After that he was not able to calm down and had to be taken back to the hospital for further treatment. His story has a happy ending. He recovered and was discharged to live a normal life a few weeks later.

One evening after fishing Dad and I were watching a patient casting from the beach. The fellow had had one arm amputated above the elbow and was good at casting with the other. He could cast beyond the drop-off at the edge of the swimming area. He managed to hold the pole against his body, turning the reel with his one hand. It was an awkward process. How would he get a fish in if he hooked one? Then we saw the answer. A big bass struck the man's lure, he pulled back to set the hook. Then he turned with pole held high in his only hand and ran across the beach, charging up the hill towards the rehab center. The fish followed, hydroplaning over the top of the water and sliding across the sand. They didn't stop until the fish had crossed the sand and reached the grass. The man looked pleased and acted as if this had been just what he expected to happen.

On the other two occasions I was in the boat. Remember Joe, the boy who had swung the sinker into my head? Well, his mother, Lenore, had come to visit. She liked fishing and was good at casting.

186

On the afternoon we were to go fishing Dad was needed at the hospital so he dropped us off to fish, saying he would pick us up later. We trolled around with no luck as the wind got stronger. Rowing was difficult in the waves and rather than continuing to row I anchored the boat. Lenore began casting and was able to do it well, despite the wind. She was a short, well-conditioned woman who stood up in the boat to cast. She was wearing a life jacket and I didn't expect anything to happen. I remained seated, casting once in a while when she was not doing so. She was enjoying herself, I sat there watching, and the wind never let up.

"I've hooked a snag," she said. "My line won't move." She pulled this way and that but the line stayed taut. Then it slowly began to move sideways. She couldn't bring the line in but it was traveling in a big arc. There must be a fish on the line. There was. It started to pull one way, then reversed and pulled the other way. Lenore managed to bring the fish a little closer each time. It seemed near the boat but we could not see it and she could not bring it up from the bottom. I pulled up the anchor to avoid having her line tangle with the rope. Maybe the moving boat helped bring the fish up, maybe it was tired. When I saw the fish I knew it was too big for the net we had been using to land pike. Lenore reeled in more line and the fish was next to the boat. I grabbed it. It was slippery and my thumb slid into its gills, making it possible for me to slide the fish over the side and into the boat. Now it was flopping all over the bottom of the boat, the hook came out and I struggled to keep it from jumping back out. I picked up the anchor and bashed it in the head, stunning it. Lenore handed me a metal stringer and I slid one end through the gills and out the mouth of the fish, snapped it shut and fastened the stringer to the oarlock. We did not put the fish back in the water as we usually did with smaller ones.

I started rowing back with the fish slapping its tail and flopping in the boat. Dad was waiting on the beach when we got there. When he saw the fish he got excited as he had when I brought the big turtle home. But this time I had been hurt. Pike's gills are filled with little sharp teeth and my thumb was badly shredded. After tetanus shots and a few days to heal my thumb was fine. The fish weighed 12 pounds.

This time Dad had his own ideas about the head. He cut it off and put it into a bottle filled with formaldehyde. He was going to give it to Lenore as a souvenir. Turned out she did not want it so we ended up with the fish head in a bottle. Not many people have one of those.

My cousin, Gary, came to visit later that summer. Let me set the scene.

Both Gary and I were a lot bigger than when we had taken a boat out in East Harbor. Gary was about 6'3" and 210 lbs. and was an experienced fisherman. Every summer his family had taken a two-week vacation at a good fishing lake in Michigan. In addition Gary had competed in casting contests in Toledo where the goal was to drop your cast into a floating ring about 30" in diameter. The difficulty increased as the ring moved farther away.

Gary had traveled to Battle Creek by bus, carrying his prize winning, 7' all–in–one–piece casting rod. It could not be broken down into two or three pieces and attracted a lot of attention. He was ready to go fishing.

Gary and I went out to Eagle Lake the next morning. We were casting in good spots but had no strikes. When we reached where Lenore had caught her fish we anchored. After a few casts Gary said, "I've got something heavy on my line." It didn't maneuver like a fish but resisted as Gary pulled it in. When it surfaced several feet from the boat we saw it was a huge turtle. We didn't want it in the boat and didn't want to cut the line. We decided to drag it to the beach, not knowing what we would do then. About halfway to shore the turtle suddenly let go and disappeared. No turtle soup this time.

The next day Dad was with us. He was in front, I was in the middle and Gary in the back. We had trolled most of the way around the lake, I had caught a small pike. Not wanting to go around again we anchored off shore at the far end of the lake.

We were admiring how far Gary could cast when he got a strike. The fish jumped out of the water. We could tell it was a big pike. Gary was doing well bringing it in. We could see it clearly in the water near the surface. Then suddenly the fish dove deep and headed back out. Gary was scared and afraid he would lose the fish. Dad told him to apply drag to slow the fish. This worked but the pike was now father away than it had been in the beginning.

This time Gary kept his rod in an upright position ready to counter any attempt by the pike to run away. There were several times when the rod bent so much the tip was no higher than Gary's hands. Each time, with the rod absorbing part of the fish's energy, Gary was able to meet the challenge. This time Gary worked the fish up to the boat.

Now all we had to do was get it in the boat. Dad handed me a gaff hook he had bought after my experience with Lenore's fish. My first effort with the gaff hook failed. Although the point of the hook was sharp I didn't pull it up hard enough to penetrate the pike's scales and skin. The next time I jerked the hook up aggressively. The gaff hook didn't penetrate this time either but went up one side of the fish with the shank going up the other side. This time I didn't stop pulling. With Gary lifting the front of the fish and me pulling up the middle, the fish landed into the boat as 'fisherman's luck' would have it.

The three of us sat there, watching it flop around. It was still hooked and when we attached it to our stringer the battle was over. We discussed who was going to take the hook out of the pike's mouth. It was decided to leave it in, stop fishing and go home for the day. (You need a pair of long nosed pliers in your tackle box for extracting hooks.)

This pike weighed eight pounds. We saved the head to dry on a nail at the back of the garage, no formaldehyde. Bees came around and ate the meat off the skull. The skin dried in the sun. We propped the fish's mouth wide open thereby showing impressive rows of big sharp teeth. (I still have this fish head on display.)

The next two discussions pertain to the 'art of fishing', not to the drama of catching a Big One.

After the lakes around Battle Creek froze over with at least three or four inches of ice Dad and I went ice fishing. This entailed using a "spud" to chop a hole in the ice. Sometimes we chopped several holes in an attempt to find where the fish were. Although we managed to catch a few pan fish once in awhile, it took persistence because it was so cold out there. We didn't have an ice shanty and our hands and feet got cold in less than an hour. Even so we enjoyed the opportunity to get a line in the water.

I recall an incident from one of our expeditions onto the ice. Dad and I, along with Dr. Albright, an old time family friend, had been out on the ice for more than an hour without catching any fish. Dr. Albright said, "I'm getting cold and restless. You keep fishing, I'm going to take a walk around the lake and see if I can fall in." He was joking of course. After a while we heard him shouting, "Help, I need help!" He had broken through the ice near shore into water about two feet deep. By the time we reached him, Dr. Albright was shaking dramatically. He had managed to find a patch of stronger ice and climb out. Dad rushed him to the car, took off his wet clothes, wrapped him in blankets and started the car heater. I went back and gathered our gear.

We drove to Dr. Albright's house and by the time we arrived he had stopped shaking but was still cold. He got into bed and warmed up under several covers. We had had a scare but he was okay, and we all agreed that it was not a joking matter, and could have been much worse.

My second story is about catching the "limit" in fishing. At that time Michigan had fishing laws that set a limit of five on the number of black bass you could catch in one day. Any bass less than ten inches long had to be unhooked and returned to the water. With Dad's help, encouragement, and especially pressure, I caught the limit one evening on a small lake at Ft. Custer. We had tried to catch fish before in the same lake. The water was clear and we could see many black bass about ten inches long. We had managed to catch one or two on occasion but it was not easy. The fish seemed smarter or more wary than fish in other lakes.

I got caught up in the challenge they presented and started thinking about their behavior. I observed that they would not bite if they could see you, or if you could see them. I tested this theory by casting from an open spot on the shore where they could easily see me. No matter what bait or lure I used I could not get a strike. They would not bite if they could see my shadow on the water.

So I tried standing well back from the shore and casting from a spot where I could not see the fish and my shadow did not reach the water. But there were still issues to resolve. What lure should I use? What time of day did they feed?

After some more trial and error I determined that these fish fed near dusk and were attracted by a lure called a "flat fish". Also, the flat fish had to float on the surface and be reeled in slowly so that the lure would not dive down below the surface of the water.

This combination of procedures proved to work well on the next few times we fished that lake. Dad was impressed and wouldn't fish while I was using my technique. I was usually ready to quit after I had caught two or three bass, enough for dinner. And too, the mosquitoes came out at dusk and attacked me. But Dad wanted me to keep fishing until I had caught my "limit" and he planned a fishing trip around that idea.

This put pressure on me and I was not used to it. I liked to bring home something to talk about and then eat, without any specifications about type or size or number of fish caught. I didn't look forward to this trip as an adventure and felt I had to prove I could do it.

We went to the lake just before dusk. Dad didn't even bring his fishing pole. I did pretty well, catching three keepers quickly. Then things slowed down. I moved to a different spot and caught one too small to keep. Then I caught one barely ten inches long. One more to go. It got darker, mosquitoes were thick and kept me swatting between casts. It was hard to turn the reel slowly and steadily with the mosquitoes biting me. I told Dad I was ready to quit if he was. He wasn't ready. He told me to persist, that I was close to the goal and shouldn't quit before he and I had something to brag about. I ended up wanting to get it done so we wouldn't have to come back again.

It was dark when I finally caught another bass over ten inches. I was glad it was over. I felt I didn't need to do it again. I had demonstrated to both of us that I understood the art of fishing well enough to pass my knowledge on to others.

Concluding Remarks

In hindsight, this essay is about growing up with Mom and Dad. When faced with a challenge, Dad had an uncanny ability to tell you immediately what needed to be done to change that challenge into an opportunity. For example, "You can't catch a fish without a line in the water." In reaction to this kind of statement, Mom would say, "Dad's an incurable optimist." Nevertheless she liked to go fishing and enjoyed cooking and eating fish. She was optimistic about having a good time during the whole process of going fishing.

Dad's optimism had made the idea of going fishing more enticing. If I suggested it was time to go fishing and Dad hesitated for a moment, I would say the magic words ("You can't etc."). Often this overrode the reason for hesitating and we went fishing. It is difficult to counter your own optimism with pessimistic thoughts. Sometimes the situation was reversed and Dad did this to me. In later years I have used those same magic words about fishing to encourage others to take an opportunity rather than to hesitate when it is something they want to do.

Shortly after I finished high school Dad was ordered to Washington, DC, to become Chief of the Medical Department at Walter Reed Army Hospital. I went to the University of Michigan that fall (1949). I met Mary there and fell (that's a strange way to put it) in love with her. Part of our courtship involved catching night crawlers just in front of third base at Fisher Stadium, the University of Michigan baseball field. There weren't any lights there in those days and it was not locked up as it is now. It was a good, quiet, dark place to catch night crawlers. Anyhow the point is I had started to use what I had learned about fishing to show others how to do it. I was on my own now.

Not realizing it then, I was taking a leadership role. A year or so ago one of our four daughters sent me a book which had a definition of leadership used by the Coast Guard Academy: "Leadership is the ability to reconcile opportunity and competency." If I were to continue these memoirs, the title of the section after "Challenges to Opportunities" would be "Opportunity and Competency." It might cover the period from 1954 to now, but a third generation is growing up now. And the spirit of fishing has not died out.

We had a reunion in 2012 on a lake in New York State where my daughter and her husband own two houses. Mary and I were both born in 1932 and the purpose of the reunion was to celebrate our 80th birthdays. On this occasion we went fishing, we caught enough perch and a pike to have fish for dinner.

As a present I gave each daughter a fish head to remember the event. Those fish heads had been hanging in the garage for 30 years. You can do this if you have lived in the same house since 1960. They came from one of our many summer vacations at Bear Lake when all four daughters were still living with us. By the way, there are lots of lakes named Bear Lake in Michigan. This is the one next to Cub Lake.

It is cold in Ann Arbor today and I have no plans to go ice fishing this winter. But looking forward to next summer, I do plan to get a line in the water at another Bear Lake, this one close to Lake Michigan.

Gary Snyder

Gary is a preeminent environmentalist, poet/writer, and thinker making his current home on the West Coast.

WRITERS AND THE WAR AGAINST NATURE

I grew up in the maritime Pacific northwest, on a farm north of Seattle where we kept a hen flock, had a small orchard and tended dairy cows. My uncles were loggers, merchant seamen, or fishermen.

After college, where I studied Anthropology, literature and East Asian culture, I had no choice but to go back to working in the woods and at sea. In the late fifties I worked in the engine room on an American-flag oil tanker that hired me out of the port of Yokohama. I was a member of the National Maritime Union, had my seaman's papers, and it wasn't hard to pick up a job in almost any port of the world. That ship kept me at sea for a continuous nine months. Two things touched me deeply on that job: one was the stars, night after night, at every latitude, including way below the equator. With my little star book and red-beam flashlight I mastered the constellations of the southern hemisphere. The other was getting to know the birds of the ocean. I loved watching the albatross – a few of those huge graceful birds would always be cruising along behind our ship, trailing the wake for bits of food. I learned that a Wandering Albatross (of the southern hemisphere) might fly a million miles in one lifetime, and that it takes a pair of them almost a year to raise one chick. Night and day, they always followed us, and if they ever slept it seems it was on the wing.

Last January a study was released describing the sudden decline of albatross numbers worldwide. It even prompted an editorial in the New York Times (January 20, 2005). This sharp decline is attributed to much death by drowning. The long-line fishing boats lay out lines with bait and hooks that go miles back, dragging just below the surface. An albatross will go for the bait, get hooked and be pulled down to drown. As many as 100,000 a year are estimated to perish in this way, enough to threaten the survival of the species if it keeps up. What have the albatross, "Distinguished strangers who have come down to us from another world," ever done to us? The editorial concludes, "The long-line fishing fleet is over-harvesting the air as well as the sea."

Out on the South Pacific in 1958, watching the soaring albatrosses from the stern of a ship, I could never have guessed that their lives would be threatened by industrial societies, turning them into "collateral damage" of the affluent appetite for *ahi* and *maguro* tuna species (my own taste too). Yet this is just a tiny, almost insignificant, example of the long reach of the globalized economy and the consumer society into the wild earth's remote places. A recent book on global logging and deforestation is titled *Strangely Like War*. What is happening now to nature worldwide, plant life and wildlife, ocean, grassland, forest, savannah, desert – all spaces and habitats – the non-human realm of watersheds and ecosystems with all their members, can be likened to a war against nature.

Although human beings have interacted with nature – both cultivated and wild, for millennia, and sometimes destructively so, it was never quite like "war." It has now become disconcertingly so, and the active defense of nature has been joined by a few artists and writers who have entered the fight on "the wild side" along with subsistence peoples, indigenous spiritual leaders, many courageous scientists, and conservationists and environmentalists worldwide.

There is a tame, and also a wild, side to the human mind. The tame side, like a farmer's field, has been disciplined and cultivated to produce a desired yield. It is useful, but limited. The wild side is larger, deeper, more complex, and though it cannot be fully known, it can be explored. The explorers of the wild mind are often writers and artists. The "poetic imagination" of which William Blake so eloquently spoke, is the territory of wild mind. It has landscapes and creatures within it that will surprise us, it can refresh us and scare us; it reflects the larger truth of our ancient selves, both animal and spiritual.

The French anthropologist Claude Levi-Strauss once said something like, "Art survives within modern civilization rather like little islands of wilderness saved to show us where we came from." Someone else once said that what makes writing good is the wildness in it. The wildness gives heart, courage, love, spirit, danger, compassion, skill, fierceness and sweetness – all at once – to language. From ancient times storytellers, poets, and dramatists have presented the world in all its fullness: plants, animals, men and women, changing shape – speaking multiple languages – inter-marrying – traveling to the sky and under the earth. The great myths and folktales of human magic and nature's power were our school for ten thousand years. Whether they know it or not, even modern writers draw strength from the wild side.

How can artists and writers manage to join in the defense of the planet and wild nature? Writers and artists by their very work "bear witness." They don't wield financial, governmental, or military power. However, at the outset they were given, as in fairy tales, two "magic gifts": One is the "Mirror of Truth." Whatever they hold this mirror up to is shown in its actual form, and the truth must come out. May we use that mirror well! The second is a "Heart of Compassion," which is to say the ability to feel and know the pains and delights of other people, and to weave that feeling into their art. For some this compassion can extend to all creatures and to the world itself. In a way, nature even borrows the voices of some writers and artists. Anciently this was a shamanistic role where the singer, dancer, or storyteller embodied a force, appearing as a bear dancer or a crane dancer, and became one with a spirit or creature. Today, such a role is played by the writer who finds herself a spokesperson for non-human entities communicating to the human realm through dance or song. This could be called "speaking on behalf of nature" in the old way.

Song, story, and dance are fundamental to all later "civilized" literature. In archaic times these were unified in dramatic performance, back when drama and religious ceremony were still one. They are reunited today in the highest and greatest of performance arts – the grand scale of European opera, the height of ballet, the spare and disciplined elegance of Japanese Nô theater, the grand and almost timeless dance-and-story of Indonesian Gamelan, the wit and hardiness of Bertolt Brecht's plays, or the fierce and stunningly beautiful intensity of Korean P'ansori performance. Performance is of key importance because this phenomenal world and all life is of itself, "not a book, but a performance." I will say more about performance a little further on.

For a writer or artist to become an advocate for nature, he or she must first stumble into some connection to that vast world of energies and ecologies. Because I was brought up in a remote rural district, instead of having kids to play with I had to entertain myself by exploring the forest surrounding our farm, observing the dozens of bird species and occasional deer, fox, or bobcat; sometimes hunting, sometimes gathering plants that I could sell to herb-buyers for a few pennies, and camping out alone for several days at a time. Heavy logging was going on in the nearby hills. Even as a boy I was deeply troubled by the destruction of the forests and the careless way that hunting – both of waterfowl and deer – was conducted.

At fifteen I got into the higher mountains of the Cascade Range in Washington State, starting with the ridges and high meadows around the snow-covered volcano called Mt. St. Helens, or Luwit, a 3000-meter peak just north of the Columbia River. Here is what I discovered back then, and finally chose to write about in my recent book *Danger on Peaks*.

Climbing the Mountain

Reaching the summit, I thought – West Coast snowpeaks are too much! They are too far above the surrounding lands, there is a break between, they are in a different world. If you want to get a view of the world you live in, climb a little rocky mountain with a neat small peak. The big snowpeaks pierce the realm of clouds and cranes, rest in the zone of five-colored banners and writhing crackling dragons in veils of ragged mist and frost-crystals, of pure transparency in blue.

Mt St. Helens' summit is smooth and broad, a place to nap, to sit and write, watch what's higher in the sky, or do a little dance. Whatever the numbers say, snowpeaks are always far higher than the highest airplanes ever get. I made my petition to the perfect shapely mountain, "Please help this life." When I tried to look over and down to the world below, there was nothing there.

And then we grouped up to descend. The afternoon snow was perfect for glissade, and leaning on our stocks we slid and skid between cracks and thumps into soft snow, dodged lava slabs, got into the open snowfield slopes and almost flew to the soft pumice slopes below. Coming down is so fast – still high we walked the three-mile dirt road back to the lake.

Atomic Dawn

The day I first climbed Mount St. Helens was August 13, 1945.

Spirit Lake was far from the cities of the valley, and news came slow. Though the first atomic bomb was dropped on Hiroshima August 6, and the second dropped on Nagasaki August 9, photographs didn't appear in the Portland Oregonian until August 12. Those papers must have been driven in to Spirit Lake on the 13th. Early the morning of the 14th I walked over to the lodge to check the bulletin board. There were whole pages of the paper pinned up: photos of a blasted city from the air, the estimate of 150,000 dead in Hiroshima alone, the American scientist quoted saying, "Nothing will grow there again for seventy years." The morning sun on my shoulders, the fir forest smell and the big tree shadows; my feet in thin moccasins feeling the ground, and my heart still one with the snowpeak mountain at my back. Horrified, blaming scientists and politicians and the governments of the world, I swore a vow to myself something like "By the purity and beauty and permanence of Mt. St. Helens, I swear I will fight against this cruel destructive power and those who would seek to use it, for all my life."

The statement in that 1945 newspaper saying that nature would be blighted for decades to come outraged me almost as much as the destruction of innocent human life. I was already a youthful conservationist/environmentalist, and after that I went on to be active in the anti-war movement as a student, and struggled against the use and proliferation of nuclear weapons. At the time it seemed as though these efforts were naïve and hopeless, but we persevered.

During my university years I was studying the philosophies and religions of the world. I learned that the most important single ethical teaching of the Buddhist tradition is non-violence toward all of nature, Ahimsa. This seemed absolutely right to me. In the Abrahamic religions, "Thou shalt not kill" applies only to human beings. In Socialist thought as well, human beings are all-important, and with the "labor theory of value" it is as though organic nature contributes nothing of worth. Later it came to me that "green plants doing photosynthesis are the ultimate working class." Nature creates the first level of value, labor the second.

Then I read translations of Buddhist texts from India and China. The *Dao De Jing* and the *Zhuang-zi* texts helped broaden my view. I read the Lun yü – the Confucian "Analects" –and saw how the Master called for Etiquette in regard to nature, as well as human society (7.27). These studies brought me to the thought that almost all of later "high civilization" has been a type of social organization that alienates humans from their own biological and spiritual heritage.

While I was laboring in the forests most of my fellow loggers were Native Americans of the Wasco and Wishram tribes of Eastern Oregon. From them I learned that it was possible to be a hunter and a fisherman with a deep spiritual attitude of gratitude and non-violence.

Eventually I re-entered college as a graduate student in East Asian Languages at the University of California at Berkeley, and finally got a chance to go to East Asia. I lived for a while in a Zen practice hall in Kyoto, Japan, and studied with a Zen teacher in the Rinzai (Chinese Linji) tradition. I took the precepts under my teacher, who told me that "Of all the precepts, the First Precept is most important and contains the others: Ahimsa, Non-harming, Cause the Least Possible Harm." To live with that percept is a challenge – he once said to me. "How do you not harm a fence? How would you save a ghost?"

I lived in Japan for ten years, partly in the monastery, but also in my own little house, and supported myself by teaching English conversation to Japanese company people. I asked my adult students, "Why are you so intent on learning English?" They answered, "Because we intend to extend our economic influence worldwide, and English is the international language." I didn't take them seriously. Today that company, Matsushita Electric, is worldwide.

In my spare time I hiked in the local mountains, learned East Asian plants and birds, and started seriously reading scientific books on ecology and biology. All those essays analyzing food-chains and food webs – this was science, I realized, dealing with energy-exchange and the natural hierarchies of various living systems. "When energy passes through a system it tends to organize that system," someone wrote. It finally came to me that this was about "eating each other" – almost as a sacrament. I wrote my first truly ecological poem, which explores the essential qualities of human foods:

The Song of the Taste

Eating the living germs of grasses
Eating the ova of large birds
the fleshy sweetness packed
around
the sperm of swaying trees

The muscles of the flanks and thighs of
soft-voiced cows
the bounce in the lamb's leap
the swish in the ox's tail

Eating roots grown swoll
inside the soil.

Drawing on life of living
clustered points of light spun
out of space
hidden in the grape.

Eating each other's seed
eating

ah, each other.

Kissing the lover in the mouth of bread:
lip to lip.

This innocently celebratory poem went straight to the question of conflict between the ethics of Ahimsa, non-violence, "respect for all beings," and the necessary lives of indigenous peoples and Native Americans I had known. They still practice ceremonies of gratitude, and they never present themselves as superior to other life forms. Ahimsa taken too literally leaves out the life of the world, and makes the rabbit virtuous but the hawk somehow evil. We must see the organic world as a great feast, a *puja*, to which we are the invited guests, and also, sooner or later, part of the meal. We can be grateful for that. We can enter into the process, but with gratitude and care, not an arrogant assumption of human privilege. This cannot come from "thinking about" nature, it comes from a being within nature.

There are plenty of people of influence and authority in the churches, in industry, the universities, and high in government who still like to describe nature as "red in tooth and claw" (a line of Alfred Tennyson's) – a fundamental misunderstanding – and use it as part of the justification for the war against nature.

I would now like to propose some simple definitions: The English word "nature" is from Latin *natura,* "birth, constitution, character, course of things" – ultimately from *nasci,* to be born. It connects with the root *nat* which is connected with birth, so we have nation, natal, and native. The Chinese word for nature is *zi-ran,* (in Korean *jayeon*), meaning "self-thus." Although in common English and American usage "nature" is sometimes used to mean "the outdoors" and set in opposition to the realm of development, the word nature is best used in its specific scientific sense, referring to the physical universe and its rules, the "laws of nature." In this use it is equivalent to the Greek *physis*. In other words, nature means "everything." The agricultural, the urban, the wild mountains and forests, and the many stars in the sky are all equally phenomena. "Nature" is our reality.

Cities and agricultural lands however are not "wild." Wild is a valuable word. It is a term for the free and independent process of nature. A wilderness need not be a place that was never touched by humans, but simply a place where wild process has ruled for some decades.

The wild is self-creating, self-maintaining, self-propagating, self-reliant, self-actualizing, and it has no "self." It is perhaps the same as what East Asian philosophers call the Dao. The human mind, imagination, and even natural human language, can also thus be called wild. The human body itself with its circulation, respiration, and digestion is wild. In these senses wild is a word for intrinsic, non-theistic, forever-changing natural order.

Ecology, another key word, has Greek *oikos* as its main root, with the simple meaning of "household." It referred originally to the study of biological interrelationships and the flow of energy through organisms and inorganic matter. In recent years it has become a popular synonym for "outdoor nature" in popular usage. I prefer to use it closer to the original meaning, with an emphasis on the dynamics of relationship in wild natural process. (I presented these definitions more fully in my 1990 book *The Practice of the Wild*.)

The field of ecological study embraces questions of population rise and fall, plant and animal succession, predator-prey relationships, competition and cooperation, feeding levels, and the flow of energy through ecosystems – and this is just the beginning. I have learned a great deal in my work on the forest issues of western North America over the last few years from people in the field of "forest ecology" (sometimes with the help of my older son Kai Snyder, who is in this field). I have come to better understand the dynamism of natural systems, the continuous role of disturbance and the unremitting effects of climactic fluctuations. The "human ecology" aspect of the ecological sciences helps us understand the role that human beings have played as members of wild nature, and how the interconnectedness of the entire planet requires that we take care of this place that we live in, and which lives in us. It tells us what "sustainable" means, and that modern humans must again become members of the organic world.

The organic life of the planet has maintained itself, constantly changing, and has gone through and recovered from several enormous catastrophic events over hundreds of millions of years. Now we are realizing that the human impact on air, water, wildlife, soil, and plant life is so extreme that there are species becoming extinct, water dangerous even to touch, mountains with mudslides but no trees, and soil that won't grow food without the continuous subsidy provided by petroleum. As we learned over time to positively work for peace to head off the possibilities of war, so now we must work for sustainable biological practices and a faith that includes wild nature if we are to reverse the prospect of continually dwindling resources and rising human populations.

One can ask what it might take to have an agriculture that does not degrade the soils, a fishery that does not deplete the ocean, a forestry that keeps watersheds and ecosystems intact, population policies that respect human sexuality and personality while holding numbers down, and energy policies that do not set off fierce little wars. These are the key questions.

Many of our leaders assume that the track we're on will go forever and nobody will learn much; politics as usual. It's the same old engineering, business, and bureaucracy message with its lank rhetoric of data and management. Or, when the talk turns to "sustainability" the focus is on a limited ecological-engineering model that might guarantee a specific resource for a while longer (like grass, water, or trees) but lacks the vision to imagine the health of the whole planet. The ethical position that would accord intrinsic value to non-human nature, and would see human beings as involved in moral as well as practical choices in regard to the natural world, makes all the difference.

"As a dewdrop, a bubble, a cloud, a flash of lightning, view all created things." Thus ends the Diamond Sutra, reminding us of irreducible impermanence. Sustainability cannot mean some kind of permanence. A waggish commentary says, "Sustainability is a physical impossibility. But it is a very nice sentiment." The quest for permanence has always led us astray – whether building stone castles, Great Walls, Pyramids for the Kings, great navies, giant cathedrals to ease us toward heaven, or Cold War scale weapons systems guaranteeing "mutually assured destruction." We must live with change, like a bird on the wing, and doing so – let all the other beings live on too. Not permanence, but "living in harmony with the Way."

The albatross, all 16 species of them, are companions with us on earth, sailing on their own way, of no use to us humans, and we should be no use to them. They can be friends at a distance, fellow creatures in the stream of evolution. This is fundamental etiquette. Legislation from the governments regarding fisheries in the sea or deforestation in the mountains would help enormously.

So back to those key questions, what would it take? We know that Science and the Arts can be allies. We need far more women in politics. We need a religious view that embraces nature and does not fear science; business leaders who know and accept ecological and spiritual limits, political leaders who have spent time working in schools, factories, or farms and who still write poems. We need intellectual and academic leaders who have studied both history and ecology, and like to dance and cook. We need poets and novelists who pay no attention to literary critics. But what we ultimately need most is human beings who love the world.

One time in Alaska a young Koyukon Indian college student asked me, "If we humans have made such good use of animals, eating them, singing about them, drawing them, riding them, and dreaming about them, what do they get back from us?" I thought it an excellent question, directly on the point of etiquette and propriety, and putting it from the animals' side. I told her, "The Ainu say that the deer, salmon, and bear like our music and are fascinated by our languages. So we sing to the fish or the game, speak words to them, say grace. We do ceremonies and rituals. Performance is currency in the deep world's gift economy." The "deep world" is of course the thousand-million-year old world of rock, soil, water, air, and all living beings, all acting through their roles. "Currency" is what you pay your debt with. We all receive, every day, the gifts, the gifts of the Deep World, from the air we breathe to the food we eat. How do we repay that gift? Performance. "A song for your supper."

I went on to tell her that I felt that non-human nature is basically well inclined toward humanity and only wishes modern people were more reciprocal, not so bloody. The animals are drawn to us, they see us as good musicians, and they think we have cute ears. The human contribution to the planetary ecology might be our entertaining eccentricity, our skills as musicians and performers, our awe-inspiring dignity as ritualists and solemn ceremonialists – because that is what seems to delight the watching wild world.

Gift Economy, what's that? That might be another perspective on the meaning of ecology, this great potluck feast to which we are all the invited guests, and we also are eventually the meal. The Ainu of Hokkaido, when they had venison for dinner, sang songs aloud to the deer spirits who were hanging about waiting for the performance. The deer visit human beings so that they might hear some songs. In

Buddhist spiritual ecology, the first thing to give up is your ego. The ancient Vedic philosophers said that the gods like sacrifices, but of all sacrifices that which they most appreciate is your ego. This critical little point is the foundation of yogic and Buddhist askesis. Zen Philosopher Dogen famously said, "We study the self to forget the self. When you forget the self you become one with the ten thousand things." (There is only one offering that is greater than the ego, and that is "enlightenment" itself.)

The being who is willing to give away her enlightenment is called a Bodhisattva. In some of the Polynesian societies the Big Person, the most respected and powerful figure in the village, was the one who had nothing – whatever gift came to him or her was promptly given away again. This is the real heart of a Gift Economy, the economy that would save, not devour, the world. (Gandhi once said, "For greed, all of nature is insufficient.") Art takes nothing from the world, it is a gift and an exchange. It leaves the world nourished.

Poems, novels, plays, with their great deep minds of story, awaken the Heart of Compassion. And so they confound the economic markets, rattle the empires, and open us up to the actually existing human and non-human world. Performance is art in motion; in the moment; both enactment and embodiment. This is exactly what nature herself is.

> Soaring just over the sea-foam
> riding the wind of the endless waves
> albatross, out there, way
>
> away, a far cry
> down from the sky